Perpendicular height of the source of Tiber Creek above the level of the tide in said Creek. F. I. P.ts 236. 7 ½.

The water of this Creek may be conveyed on the high ground where the Capitol stands & after watering that part of the City may be destined to other useful purposes.

Perpendicular height of the ...nd where the Capitol is to ...is above the tide of Tiber Creek 78 Feet.

Perpendicular height of the West branch above the tide in Tiber Creek. F. I. P.ts 145. 7. ⅛

PLAN
of the CITY of
Washington
in the Territory of Columbia,
ceded by the States of
VIRGINIA and MARYLAND
to the
United States of America,
and by them established as the
SEAT of their GOVERNMENT,
after the Year
MDCCC.

Engrav'd by Thackara & Vallance Philad.ᵃ 1792.

Capitol

PART OF MARYLAND WITHIN THE TERRITORY OF COLUMBIA.

EASTERN BRANCH

Breadth of the Streets.

THE grand Avenues, and such Streets as lead immediately to public places, are from 130 to 160 feet wide, and may be conveniently divided into foot ways, walks of trees, and a carriage way. The other Streets are from 90 to 110 feet wide.

IN order to execute this plan, Mr. ELLICOTT drew a true Meridional line by celestial observation, which passes through the Area intended for the Capitol; this line he crossed by another due East and West, which passes through the same Area. These lines were accurately measured, and made the basis on which the whole plan was executed. He ran all the lines by a Transit Instrument, and determined the Acute Angles by actual measurement, and left nothing to the uncertainty of the Compass.

The
White House
Is Burning

August 24, 1814

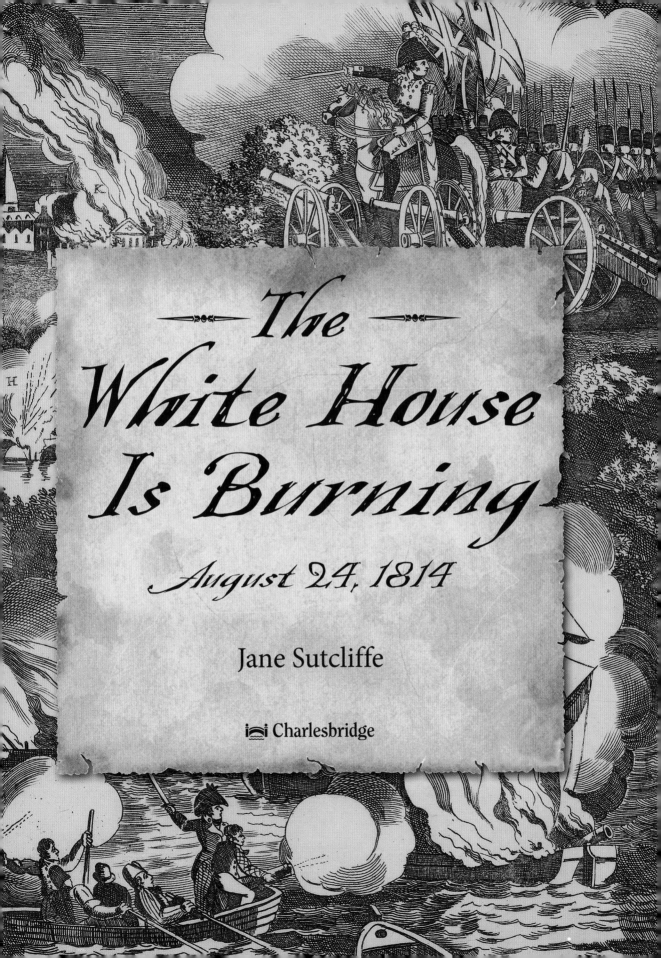

The White House Is Burning

August 24, 1814

Jane Sutcliffe

Charlesbridge

For Skip, Eileen, and Virginia, who knew when to hold my hand

Published by Charlesbridge
85 Main Street
Watertown, MA 02472
(617) 926-0329
www.charlesbridge.com

Library of Congress Cataloging-in-Publication Data
Sutcliffe, Jane.
  The White House is burning : August 24, 1814 / Jane Sutcliffe.
    pages cm
  Includes bibliographical references.
  ISBN 978-1-58089-656-6 (reinforced for library use)
  ISBN 978-1-60734-544-2 (ebook)
  ISBN 978-1-60734-654-8 (ebook pdf)
1. White House (Washington, D.C.)—History—19th century—Juvenile literature.
[1. Washington (D.C.)—History—Capture by the British, 1814—Juvenile literature.] I. Title.

E356.W3S88 2014
975.3'02—dc23   2013014226

Printed in China
(hc) 10 9 8 7 6 5 4 3 2 1

Cover illustration done in oil on prepared bristol board
Display type set in Queensland by Scriptorium Font Library
    and P22 Mayflower by Ted Staunton
Text type set in Minion Pro by Adobe Systems Incorporated
Color separations by KHL Chroma Graphics, Singapore
Printed and bound February 2014 by Jade Productions in Heyuan, Guangdong, China
Production supervision by Brian G. Walker
Designed by Diane M. Earley

Half title: The President's House, later called the White House.
Title page: A city in flames: Washington, August 24, 1814.

Contents

The unthinkable: enemy soldiers invade Washington, DC, and burn its most beloved symbols.

Introduction

Had it happened in modern times, it would have been called breaking news. Camera crews in helicopters would have covered it all, live and on the scene.

A nation would have gathered to watch the shocking images: A battle with enemy troops just outside Washington, DC. The humiliating defeat of American soldiers. Residents of Washington fleeing the city in terror. The last-minute evacuation of the First Lady from the White House. Then the unthinkable: foreign invaders marching into Washington, torching first the Capitol building, then the White House.

For weeks, months, years after, we would have watched the horrifying footage replayed over and over, the sight of flames against the night sky as the nation's capital burned.

That was the scene on August 24, 1814. Of course, there were no television cameras. There were no on-the-scene reporters. There were only those who lived through that unforgettable day. Some were important people in history: the president and his wife, the military leaders of the time. But others were ordinary people: a doctor, a clerk, a teenage soldier, a nine-year-old slave. Many of them felt moved to record that day in their diaries or letters or memoirs. Their words bring to life the shock and shame of that day.

This is what they saw.

A peaceful Washington and the hills of Georgetown.

Chapter One

The Hours Before Dawn

A Knock in the Night

For the Smith family of Washington, DC, the alarm came in the middle of the night. First came a loud banging on the door, followed by the frantic voice of a family friend.

Margaret Bayard Smith remembered:

> On the opening of the door, Willie Bradley called to us, "The enemy are advancing, our own troops are giving way on all sides and are retreating to the city. Go, for Gods sake go." . . . We immediately rose, the carriage and horses were soon ready, we loaded a wagon with what goods remained and about 3 oclock left our house with all our servants.

The Mouse and the Lion

In the summer of 1814, the United States was only thirty-eight years old, still an infant as countries go. And it was at war with the greatest superpower of the day.

The seeds of the war—today called the War of 1812—had been sown long before, in another war. For years Britain had been locked in battle with France. The United States had declared itself neutral and had tried to stay out of the fight. Instead, it found itself being used as a weapon by both countries.

First France declared it had the right to seize British goods on American ships. It also decided that American ships could not dock at French ports if they had first docked at British ones. Britain responded by requiring American ships to do just that—they had to dock at British harbors first before entering French-controlled ports. How was the United States supposed to do both?

Even worse, Britain refused to recognize a British sailor's right to renounce his citizenship and become an American sailor. The British routinely boarded American ships to seize these "deserters." They hauled off a number of native-born American sailors, too, for good measure. The sailors were forced—or "impressed"—into service to the Crown. Between 1804 and 1810 nearly 5,000 seamen were dragged from American ships, including 1,361 who had been born in the United States.

The Royal Navy called impressment its right under maritime law. The American people called it kidnapping, and they were outraged.

Along the northern frontier, settlers had their own gripes. This time it was with British officials in Canada, which belonged to Britain. They accused the officials of arming local Native Americans

The British navy saw the boarding of American ships and the taking of British-born sailors as a right. American seamen saw it as an act of war.

and inciting them to violence across the border.

To proud Americans these insults were intolerable. Hadn't their fathers fought the Revolution to be free of British interference? "War hawks" in Congress began to call for war. It was to be a second fight for independence.

On June 18, 1812, President James Madison signed a declaration of war against Britain. It was the first declaration of war for the young country, and a very bold move. Britain was at the height of its military power, especially at sea. The British navy had hundreds of warships. The United States had only eighteen.

At the last minute Britain withdrew its orders restricting trade. But the news reached Washington too late. The mouse and the lion were already at war.

Tale of a Tyrant

Most of the fighting took place far from Washington, along the Canadian border. But on the Chesapeake Bay, which lay less than fifty miles from the capital, coastal towns were also under attack. British ships swept in to terrorize citizens. Sailors under the command of Admiral George Cockburn looted private homes before burning them to the ground. The *National Intelligencer* in Washington carried shocking news of the raids:

> The enemy landed from their barges at Havre-de-Grace about sunrise. . . . They had very soon complete possession of the town, and immediately commenced plundering and burning. . . . Every thing portable was carried away. . . . The shawl was taken from Mrs. M's neck, and the child from her arms and stript of its clothing. . . . The officers, with some exceptions, were quite as greedy of plunder as the men.

Cockburn himself was singled out for his coldness and cruelty. The *National Intelligencer* called him a "monster" and a "disgrace not only to the nation, but the whole human race." The newspaper also poked fun at his name (pronounced "Coe-burn" by the British and "Cock-burn" by the Americans), nicknaming him "Houseburn." According to the *National Intelligencer*, the nickname was well earned:

> Admiral Cockburn seems to be as much despised by his own officers as he is hated by our citizens. A lady rushing by an officer, he stopped her, saying where are you going Madam? I am going to the Admiral to beg him to spare my home; save yourself the trouble Madam, that man would burn his own brother's house if he could receive any benefit from it.

Among his sailors Cockburn actually had a reputation as an outstanding seaman and tireless fighter. He was reportedly so devoted to his men that he once recommended the building of a hospital when he felt they were not receiving adequate care. But on the Chesapeake the name Cockburn became synonymous with barbarity. A reward of one thousand dollars was posted for his head, or five hundred dollars for each of his ears.

Invasion

Residents of Washington could at least console themselves with the fact that Cockburn and his men were sailors. They could not strike very far from the coast and their ships.

Then, in April 1814, the ruler of France, Napoleon Bonaparte, fell from power. Britain could now give full attention to its little war with the United States. Thousands of combat-ready, experienced soldiers were freed up for an American invasion. They would be met almost entirely by untested volunteers and local militias. The professional soldiers of the United States were widely scattered, serving anywhere from Canada to New Orleans.

By June rumors began to swirl of a large expedition in Britain being fitted out for an attack. No one was certain where the British intended to strike—maybe Philadelphia, or Baltimore, or Washington, or even all three.

On August 19, fifty-one British ships sailed from Chesapeake Bay up the Patuxent River. On board the flagship was the "monster" Cockburn. The ships carried an invasion force of four thousand five hundred soldiers—all skilled combat veterans who had embarked straight from the recent war with France. The men, under

Admiral George Cockburn in his finest moment. Behind him, Washington is in flames.

the command of General Robert Ross, were ferried ashore in rowboats at the little town of Benedict, Maryland. Then they began to march inland toward the city of Washington.

They encountered almost no resistance on the way. In fact, they met almost no one at all. The news of their approach had preceded them, and so had the waves of panic. The soldiers encountered empty towns and abandoned homes, some with bread still baking in the oven.

By the night of August 23, they had reached Upper Marlborough, Maryland, and made camp a few miles outside the town. They were less than a day's march from the capital.

"A certain James O'Boyle . . . offers a reward of 1,000 dollars for the head of the notorious incendiary and infamous scoundrel, and violator of all laws, the British Admiral Cockburn, or 500 dollars for each of his ears on delivery."

—*Niles' Register*,
August 21, 1813

"We had very little mercy to expect from Admiral Cockburn, or from those under his control, for his very name had become a terror to the people, who viewed him as a monster of cruelty."

—Christian Hines,
Washington resident

At the news of the British advance, Washington was thrown into hysteria. The Smiths were not the only family quitting the city. For days the roads had been choked with people fleeing the capital. People left in droves, with trunks and feather beds piled onto carts. That is, if they could find a cart. Government agents, desperate to move important papers to safety, confiscated anything with wheels.

A fifteen-year-old visitor from New England, known only as "Miss Brown," summed up the mood in the city: "Now all is hurry and panic, armies gathering, troops moving in all directions, the citizens trying to secure such things as were most valuable and most easily transportable, and flying from their homes to the country."

No one was immune from the panic. Eleanor Jones, wife of the secretary of the navy, had been invited to visit the White House by First Lady Dolley Madison. Mrs. Jones sent her regrets, mincing no words. She was, she said, "busy packing."

The excitement was too much for some. Bookseller Joseph Milligan fled to a friend's home in Virginia. By the time he arrived, he was shaking and gibbering in terror. He was convinced the British had chased him the whole way.

History in a Homemade Bag

About the only person in Washington who was not seeing the British over his shoulder was John Armstrong. As secretary of war, he was responsible for the military. But instead of taking command, he insisted to anyone who would listen that the city was in no danger. He refused to deploy the local militia. The head of the militia met with Armstrong and begged him to help. He pointed out that, with so many ships and men, the British clearly meant business. Obviously they meant to strike a serious blow somewhere.

"Oh yes!" Armstrong replied. "By [God], they would not come with such a fleet without meaning to strike somewhere, but they certainly will not come here; what the [devil] will they do here. . . . No, no! Baltimore is the place, sir; that is of so much more consequence."

He listened to no one, refused to heed any warning, and would not take the smallest precaution, even to safeguard national treasures. At the State Department, clerk Stephen Pleasonton had received orders to remove the office's important documents. He bought some linen cloth and had it sewn into bags. As he was placing the books and papers into the bags, Armstrong saw him. Pleasonton later described the encounter:

> Genl. Armstrong . . . stopped a short time, and observed to me that he thought we were under unnecessary alarm, as he did not think the British were serious in their intentions of coming to Washington. I replied that we were under a different belief, and let their intentions be what they might, it was the part of prudence to preserve the valuable papers of the Revolutionary Government.

He had reason to press the point. Among the precious contents of the homemade bags were the Declaration of Independence, the Constitution, and the letters of George Washington.

Flight

Awakened in the night and fleeing their home, the little Smith daughters found all the hubbub great fun. At their age anything new was an adventure. They were delighted with the hurried packing and the unexpected journey in the middle of the night.

Margaret Smith, walking in the dark beside her girls, let them giggle. She herself felt strangely calm. Even as she was leaving her home and her city, it was still unthinkable to her that the American army could be defeated and that the British would seize the capital.

She had no way of knowing that in just hours the capital would be in flames.

To War in Pumps

At the same time that the Smith family was leaving Washington, eighteen-year-old Private John Pendleton Kennedy was sleepily stumbling toward it. A volunteer soldier with the Fifth Regiment Maryland Militia, he had left home three days before in a spectacular dress parade.

"As we moved through the streets," he recalled, "the pavements were crowded with anxious spectators; the windows were filled with women; . . . the populace were cheering and huzzaing at every corner. . . . What a scene it was, and what a proud actor I was in it! . . . This was a real army marching to real war."

The young private was especially proud of his "very dashy uniform" of blue and red, and his leather helmet topped with two huge feathers.

Among the blankets and shirts in his knapsack, the young man had carefully packed a pair of men's "pumps"—fancy cloth shoes, a bit like slippers. These were needed because, he said, "after we had beaten the British army and saved Washington, Mr. Madison would very likely invite us to a ball at the White House, and I wanted to be ready for it."

By the night of August 23, the men had reached the village of Bladensburg, four miles from the capital. There was plenty of talk of a battle the next day, and Kennedy was so excited he could barely sleep. Finally drifting off around midnight, he was awakened less than an hour later by the sound of gunshots and the long roll of drums sounding an alarm. Kennedy described the chaos that ensued:

> Every one believed that the enemy was upon us, and there was consequently an immense bustle in getting ready to meet him. We struck a light to be able to find our coats,

accoutrements, etc., but in a moment it was stolen away. . . . This gave rise to some ludicrous distresses. Some got the wrong boots, others a coat that didn't fit, and some could not find their cross-belts.

In the confusion Kennedy was forced to line up with the fancy pumps on his feet.

The alarm turned out to be a false one. The private had just lain down to sleep once more when, around three o'clock, the drums rolled again.

This time it was no false alarm. The men were ordered to break camp at once. The enemy was close. The rest of the army had already retreated toward Washington. They would have to hurry to a better position closer to the capital.

There was a mad scramble to get all the gear into a wagon— knapsacks, provisions, blankets. In all the confusion, in, too, went Private Kennedy's boots. Half an hour later he was groggily dragging himself toward the capital, wearing his pumps. He had never felt so sleepy in his life:

> We had been too much exhilarated in the early part of the night to feel the fatigue of our day's march, but now that fatigue returned upon me with double force. . . . I slept as I walked. At every halt of a moment whole platoons laid down in the dusty road and slept till the officers gave the word to move on.

At last the exhausted soldiers were led into the stubble of a hay field and allowed to rest until daybreak. Kennedy threw himself onto the dew-soaked ground and fell instantly asleep. On his feet he still wore the elegant pumps.

John Pendleton Kennedy joined the Maryland Militia at age eighteen, in part to escape the drudgery of studying law as his father wanted.

Discussion in the Dark

As Margaret Smith was tossing belongings into a cart and Private Kennedy was grumbling over his false alarm, Lieutenant James Scott of the British Royal Navy was pretty sure he was lost. Aide-de-camp to Admiral Cockburn, he was carrying an urgent message from the commander in chief, Admiral Alexander Cochrane. So far Scott had made it to the town of Upper Marlborough. He knew that Cockburn and General Ross had to be nearby. But still there was no sign of the British camp, and Scott was beginning to suspect he had taken the wrong road. He was more than a little relieved when, around two in the morning, he spied the flicker of campfires through the trees.

He found the officers in a shepherd's hut, asleep on their cloaks. They woke immediately upon his arrival, and Scott handed them the commander in chief's order. He waited while first Cockburn, then Ross, read it.

Scott himself already knew the letter's contents by heart. Admiral Cochrane had ordered him to memorize the message and to destroy it if he fell into enemy hands. Scott knew, too, that Cockburn was expecting to receive the go-ahead for the invasion of Washington. What he read now must have stunned him.

> The orders contained in that letter were to the following effect: . . . that [Cockburn] was on no account to proceed one mile farther, but, upon the receipt of that order, the army was immediately to return to Benedict to re-embark; that the ulterior and principal objects of the expedition would be risked by an attempt upon the capital . . . ;—and concluded with a reiteration of the orders to return immediately.

This was a bitter blow! Cockburn had had his eye fixed on the prize of Washington from the start. Everything he had done until now was just baby steps leading to that triumph.

He wanted badly to avenge the city of York in Upper Canada, where American troops were said to have burned government buildings, including the parliament house. But even more, he knew that the capture of a capital was always a humiliating blow to a country. Such a blow might even break the young country entirely and return it to the Crown. If all went well, the so-called United States of America would cease to be a country at all and would become once again a colony of England. In time, history would forget that it had ever been an independent nation.

While Cockburn silently seethed, Ross finished reading the letter. He pointed out that they had no alternative: they had to return.

But Cockburn could not think of such a thing. "No," he replied, "we cannot do that; we are too far advanced to think of a retreat."

He proposed they take a walk and talk it over. He tried to persuade the reluctant Ross that the wisest course was to continue. Scott, a short distance away, could not help but overhear the admiral's fiery words:

> I'll pledge everything that is dear to me as an officer that we shall succeed. If we return without striking a blow, it will be worse than a defeat—it will bring a stain upon our arms. I know their force—the militia, however great their numbers, will not—cannot stand against your disciplined troops. . . . We must go on.

The discussion seesawed back and forth for hours.

As the first light colored the eastern sky, the Smith family stopped for breakfast before continuing their journey. Private Kennedy slept on in his stubbly hay field. And the two British officers at last came to a decision. General Ross agreed to Admiral Cockburn's plan. They would disobey orders. The attack of Washington was on.

Dolley Madison was as beloved as she was beautiful.

Chapter Two

Dawn

The Lady with the Spyglass

First Lady Dolley Madison was up with the sun. It could not have been an easy night. As commander in chief, her husband James had gone to join the troops on the battlefield, and she was left to pace and fret. The previous day she had started a letter to her sister Lucy in Kentucky. With every scratch of her pen, she'd poured out her fears.

> Dear Sister, My husband left me yesterday morning to join General Winder. He inquired anxiously whether I had courage or firmness to remain in the President's house until his return on the morrow, or succeeding day, and on my assurance that I had no fear but for him, and the success of our army, he left,

beseeching me to take care of myself, and of the Cabinet papers, public and private.

Now at dawn she was still waiting. With spyglass in hand she took up position on the top floor of the White House. In the weak morning light, she studied the roads, searching the shadows for any sign of her husband. In the past few days, those roads had been filled with people, horses, and carts in a frantic, noisy scramble to escape the city. Now the capital was nearly deserted. She was all but alone. Only the bustle of a few servants and the squawking of her pet macaw, Polly, broke the stillness in the house. In the previous days one hundred men had been stationed around the White House as guards. Now even they had fled.

Dolley had done as James had asked. She had filled trunks with all the important government papers in the house. Enough to fill her carriage, she wrote Lucy. But all their private things would have to be left behind. There were simply no carts left in the city to transport them.

Already the mayor of Washington had come by twice to plead with her to escape while she still could. But she could not think of leaving until she knew that James was safe. And so she waited and watched.

The Oddest Couple

In 1814 the term "First Lady" had not yet come into use to refer to the president's wife. On the occasion of James's inauguration, the *National Intelligencer* had called Dolley the "Presidentess." "Lady President" and "Lady Presidentess" were also tried out. To many, though, Dolley Madison filled the role of queen of the United States.

She was beautiful. Tall—five feet, seven and three-quarters inches—with a shapely figure and a pretty face framed by dark brown curls, she had been beautiful enough as a girl to turn heads in the street. As a young widow of twenty-six, she had turned James Madison's. The congressman had spotted Dolley on a street in Philadelphia and had asked a friend to introduce him. A few months later they were married.

They must have made an odd-looking couple. James was seventeen years older than Dolley, and at five feet six, so short that he had a number of nicknames. "Little Jemmy" was the kindest, "Pygmy" the cruelest. He dressed only in black and had a habit of combing over his powdered hair to hide his receding hairline. He was pale and frail-looking, and at his own inauguration he trembled so badly that no one could hear him speak. He was also brilliant, brainy, and bookish. In modern times James Madison would have been called a nerd.

But he was the nerd who had captured Dolley's heart. Whatever their physical differences, they were a devoted couple. "Our hearts understand each other," she told him. She called James "my beloved." His love letters to her began "My dearest."

Dolley was as outgoing as her husband was serious. She was at her best surrounded by people, and nearly everyone was charmed by her. At the inauguration party, people crowded into Long's Hotel to see not the new president, but Dolley.

> "She really in manners and appearance, answered all my ideas of royalty."
> —Margaret Bayard Smith

> "I never saw a Lady who enjoyed society more than she does. The more she has round her the happier she appears to be."
> —Catharine Akerly Mitchill, wife of Congressman Samuel Mitchill

James Madison was already famous as the "Father of the Constitution" when he was elected president in 1808.

Margaret Smith had been there: "It was scarcely possible to elbow your way from one side to another, and poor Mrs. Madison was almost pressed to death, for every one crowded round her, those behind pressing on those before, and peeping over their shoulders to have a peep of her, and those who were so fortunate as to get near enough to speak to her were happy indeed." Eventually the room became so stuffy that the windows had to be smashed to let in some air.

At a Fourth of July celebration, the teenage tourist Miss Brown was clearly starstruck by the "Presidentess":

> As we entered she was crossing the crowded vestibule, conducted by two fair girls, one on each side. . . . She stopped to receive our greetings, and that gave me time to admire the tasteful simplicity of her dress. White—but of what material I forget. Her hair hung in ringlets on each side of her face, surmounted by the snowy folds of her unvarying turban, ornamented on one side by a few heads of green wheat. She may have worn jewels, but if she did they were so eclipsed by her inherent charms as to be unnoticed.

More than one fan remarked on her simple elegance. Dolley loved fashion, but she never went overboard, with the exception of her trademark turbans. These were usually topped with flamboyant feathers so tall they bobbed over her husband's head.

Dolley's popularity allowed her to get away with a lot. In an age when women were judged harshly, she wore makeup, used snuff (tobacco), and gambled at cards. Few seemed to mind. Her secret was simple. When a congressman once told her admiringly, "Everybody loves Mrs. Madison," she replied that that was because "Mrs. Madison loves everybody."

Wednesday "Squeezes"

Every Wednesday evening, carriages left boardinghouses and hotels all over Washington. As if drawn by a magnet, they all made their way over rutted dirt roads to the President's House, now beginning to be known by its nickname, the White House. In Washington there was only one place to be on a Wednesday: Dolley Madison's drawing room.

Everyone went to "Mrs. Madison's Wednesdays." Carriage drivers let their passengers off, parked the carriage, and then went inside to sample the punch and ice cream. There they rubbed elbows—literally—with foreign diplomats, senators, and judges, as well as local shopkeepers and tourists to the city. At first, invitations appeared in the local papers. But as word spread, these were no longer necessary. People just showed up.

Dolley had created the perfect setting for her Wednesday get-togethers. Three rooms were set aside for entertaining, and each room opened into the next. In the dining room, guests were awed by the full-length painting of George Washington in its heavy gilded frame. That room led into a smaller one, known as "Mrs. Madison's parlor." Done all in sunny sunflower yellow, it featured a piano and Dolley's special find, a guitar—an uncommon sight in Washington at the time. The oval drawing room was the largest. This was Dolley's masterpiece. The cream-colored walls glowed by candlelight. Mirrors shimmered. Yards of red velvet draped the floor-to-ceiling windows. Dolley had fought hard for those curtains. Her decorator, the famous architect Benjamin Henry Latrobe, had thought they would overpower the room. But Dolley had been right. They added just the right touch of elegance.

Dolley's Wednesdays were by no means starchy formal affairs. Other presidents and first ladies had held functions at which guests stood around waiting to be greeted officially. Dolley's gatherings were more like modern parties. She let people mingle. She moved about the room and chatted with each guest as if with an old friend. Writer Washington Irving, attending one of her Wednesdays, marveled that she had "a smile and a pleasant word for everybody."

Of course, some guests huddled in corners, talking politics. Washington was, after all, a town full of politicians. Dolley's Wednesdays brought together even quarrelsome political enemies. There they could argue, make deals, and come to new agreements, all in a friendly setting. Dolley was there to charm them. And clever James was there to persuade them to see things his way.

Dolley's Wednesdays became so popular that sometimes there were two to three hundred people packed into her rooms. At one New Year's Day gathering, it got so hot that the ladies' makeup ran down their faces. People began calling her parties "squeezes." In the crush of bodies, the little president sometimes seemed to get lost. Not Dolley. Everyone always knew where she was by the feathers nodding above the heads of the crowd.

> "The windows are nearly the height of the room, and have superb red silk velvet curtains which cost $4.00 a yard."
>
> —Elbridge Gerry Jr.,
> son of the vice president

> "I was beaten by Mr. and Mrs. Madison. I might have had a better chance had I faced Mr. Madison alone."
>
> —Charles Cotesworth Pinckney,
> political opponent

The Beauty and the Brute

Dolley continued to turn her spyglass in every direction. The previous day James had written to her from the battlefield. He tried to calm her fears of invasion:

> The reports as to the enemy have varied every hour. The last
> & probably truest information is that they are not very strong,
> and are without cavalry and artillery; and of course that they
> are not in a condition to strike at Washington. It is believed
> also that they are not about to move from Marlbro', unless it
> be from an apprehension of our gathering force, and on a re-
> treat to their ships.

He snuck in a little bad news: "It is possible however they may have a greater force or expect one, than has been represented."

Since then she had had two messages from him, written in pencil and far less reassuring. "The last is alarming," she told Lucy, "because he desires I should be ready at a moment's warning to enter my carriage, and leave the city; that the enemy seemed stronger than had at first been reported, and it might happen that they would reach the city with the intention of destroying it."

"Would reach the city." How those words must have made her hand tremble as she held the spyglass to her eye. She well knew Admiral Cockburn's reputation. She knew, too, that he had more than once made his threats personal. The year before, as he was terrorizing towns along the Chesapeake, he had boasted that he would soon "make his bow" in her drawing room. More recently he had sent word to Dolley that "unless she should leave, the house would be burned over her head." Worst of all, there were rumors that he had threatened to take her prisoner and parade her through the streets of London as a prize of war.

Through it all, Dolley refused to be ruled by fear. She wrote to her cousin that she felt more offended than frightened by Cockburn's boasts. But in the same letter, she admitted, "I . . . keep the old Tunisian sabre within reach."

Still, she did not mention to Lucy her fears for herself. Her concern was for James: "I am determined not to go myself until I see Mr. Madison safe."

Target: Washington

As Dolley watched anxiously for James, three brigades of British soldiers were already in full march. During the night a rumor that a retreat had been called had made the rounds among the men. They were standing ready at dawn when the order was given to move forward—toward Washington. The drums began to roll. At the sound, a murmur of enthusiasm swept through the ranks.

Riding a white horse and wearing a gold-laced hat and epaulettes, Admiral Cockburn was dressed for glory. He was finally on his way to burn Washington. In Admiral Cochrane's words, Cockburn was out to give the former colony "a complete drubbing." He was heading toward Washington, the White House, and Dolley Madison.

George Gleig carried his journal with him to war and wrote in it daily.

Chapter Three

Morning

The View from the Woods

It was a river of red. Forty-five hundred British soldiers, most in bright scarlet uniforms, moved through the forest. The column snaked through the trees for well over a half mile.

British officer George Gleig had been on the march since just after dawn. The trail through the woods was narrow, little more than a deer path. It allowed for only four men abreast to pass, and the tangled underbrush on either side made for slow going. But at least there was shade. Tree branches formed a leafy canopy that sheltered the men from the sun. Gleig found the morning march "cool and agreeable."

The young lieutenant was no stranger to long marches. At eighteen he was already an experienced veteran. For the last year he had fought in the war against France. Being "enthusiastically attached" to his profession, he enjoyed soldiering and was actually disappointed when the war with France ended. He was more than happy when he was immediately ordered to ship out to fight in the war against the United States. With the rest of the invasion force, he had landed at Benedict five days earlier.

After months of being cooped up at sea, he had been ready for action. "One wish, and one only, rose into my mind," he admitted, "and that was, that the Americans would afford me an opportunity, with the twenty brave men whom I commanded, to make what impression I could upon any of their [ambushes]."

He had been disappointed. Once his men succeeded in flushing one hundred fifty American soldiers hiding among the trees. But the enemy did not stand and fight: "The Americans, not waiting for our approach, retreated with all haste through a country manifestly well known to them, and were beyond our reach in ten minutes."

A few days later Gleig spotted a flash of light in the woods. He knew at once what it was: the glint of sunlight on a metal weapon. He sent his soldiers to surround the spot, and on moving closer came upon two rather startled men in black coats sitting under a tree. The two were armed with guns and bayonets. They tried to persuade the British soldiers that they were nothing more than simple country folk, out for an afternoon of squirrel hunting.

> "In these first six days of campaign, there had been no fighting, to the no small encouragement of the British."
> —Colonel Allen McClane, American officer

When Gleig asked "whether they carried bayonets to charge the squirrels, as well as muskets to shoot them, they were rather at a loss for a reply." Amid grumbles on one side and hoots of laughter on the other, Gleig had taken the two unfortunate Americans prisoner.

Hoofprints in the Dirt

Nine thirty in the morning. The British soldiers were out from under the trees now, and the sun beat down on their heads without mercy. They had no way of knowing that they had come ashore smack in the middle of a heat wave. The summer had been the hottest anyone in Washington could remember, with little or no rainfall for three weeks. Even worse than the broiling sun was the stifling humidity.

Heavy woolen uniforms stuck to sweaty skin. Each step was an effort, and soldiers began to lag behind. It didn't help that every man—officer and soldier alike—carried all his belongings on his back.

"Slung over my left shoulder," Gleig remembered, "lay a black leathern haversack, containing a spare shirt, a pair of stockings, dressing utensils, a foraging cap, three pounds of boiled pork, and two pounds and a half of sea-biscuit. On my left breast, again, rested a horn, filled with rum . . . whilst a wooden keg, for the conveyance of water, hung over my neck, on the very middle of my back."

Worst of all was the dust rising from dirt roads baked to powder by the sun. Churned up by marching feet, the dust rose into the air, coating faces, stinging eyes, and choking throats.

"I do not recollect a period of my military life during which I suffered more severely from heat and fatigue," Gleig reported. "It is not surprising that before many hours had elapsed numbers of men began to fall behind from absolute inability to keep up."

Coughing and spluttering, the men marched on. Here and there they saw signs of American encampments. There were fresh footprints and hoofprints in the road, proof that enemy troops were not far ahead. And more: "The ashes of fires not long extinguished were still smoking. Morsels of provision, bits of clothing, a firelock here and there, and numerous bundles of straw, all told a tale of troops having spent the night here."

They were getting close—only ten or twelve miles from Washington now. It seemed certain that they would at least see the enemy before dark. Spirits soared, and even tired soldiers perked up at the expectation of battle with the Americans. As a wave of exhilaration passed through the troops, the buglers sensed the change in mood. They struck up a lively march.

Which Way to Washington?

President James Madison was waiting. Several of his cabinet members and military officers had joined him at the American field headquarters, and they waited now, too. Among them was Brigadier General William Winder. The defense of the city of Washington was Winder's responsibility, and he was in over his head.

Winder had been a political choice—his uncle was the governor of Maryland—and his combat experience was slight. The previous year he had even been captured by the British and held for a time before being released. He was better known as a lawyer than a military strategist, and he knew he needed help now.

Though Winder had seven thousand men to the enemy's four thousand five hundred, only nine hundred of them were professional foot soldiers—"regulars." Another four hundred were cavalry. Most were untested militiamen who had never seen blood spilled on a battlefield. Many, like the teenage Private Kennedy, saw soldiering not as a profession but as something of a lark. They would be up against disciplined British troops hardened by combat.

As news about the British advance grew more serious, Winder

*Wrong man for the job: General William Winder had little combat experi-
ence when he was entrusted with the defense of the capital.*

sent an urgent message to Secretary of War Armstrong, asking for
his immediate advice. It was Armstrong everyone was waiting for
now, and the men were getting impatient.

From time to time, mounted scouts arrived with fresh reports on
the position of the British regulars. It was clear from their accounts
that an enormous invasion force was advancing toward the capital.
But it might still be stopped if the men could figure out which route
the British were planning to take. There was a fork in the road to
Washington. One path led to the bridge at the Navy Yard, east of the
capital. The other passed through the town of Bladensburg before

approaching Washington from the north. General Winder had already placed a large number of his militiamen near the bridge in anticipation of confronting the enemy there. For an hour the president and his advisers discussed the matter and worried over what to do.

Then a messenger arrived from the commander of the Baltimore militia. The British army was advancing toward the town of Bladensburg. Without waiting for Secretary Armstrong, General Winder set his troops marching at double time toward the town.

Winder had no sooner left when the long-awaited Armstrong arrived. He was informed of the latest intelligence, and then President Madison took him aside. A battle was probable, the president told him. Did he have any advice or plan to offer in the emergency? Armstrong's reply was chilling: "He said he had not," the president noted, "adding, that as the battle would be between Militia and regular troops, the former would be beaten."

The Dust Cloud in the Sky

The red-coated soldiers were passing through open country now. Thick stands of trees separated the fields. It was just the kind of ground where cavalry troops might have an advantage. Lieutenant Gleig noticed that the men held their breath in nervous anticipation, expecting American horsemen to charge from the groves before any of them had time to prepare. But it never happened. They saw not a single American soldier.

The men were nearing exhaustion. "We had now proceeded about nine miles," Gleig reported, "during the last four of which the sun's rays had beat continually upon us, and we had inhaled almost as great a quantity of dust as of air. Numbers of men had already fallen to the rear, and many more could with difficulty keep up; consequently, if we pushed on much farther without resting, the chances were that at least one half of the army would be left behind."

It was around ten in the morning. The men had been in full march for hours. To give the stragglers a chance to catch up, a halt was called in a shady spot near a little stream. The exhausted soldiers dropped their packs and threw themselves on the grass. Within five minutes nearly every man was asleep, including Lieutenant Gleig: "My eyes were closed before my head reached the ground."

"[The British] were so overpowered by their rapid march, that many fell dead in the road. As they passed through Bladensburg, their mouths were open gasping for breath, and their officers were driving them forward with their swords."
—*National Intelligencer*, August 31, 1814

He was still sleeping when a friend shook him—hard—to get him to wake up. Gleig pried his eyes open to see his unit marching off without him. He hurried to catch up. But no sooner had the march begun again than the hillsides were once more covered with stragglers, "some of the finest and stoutest men in the army being literally unable to go on."

Around noon Gleig noticed a dense cloud in the distance. The cloud of dust rose into the air, not more than two or three miles away. It wasn't difficult for the soldiers to guess where the cloud came from. Every man there knew that dust well. It was the same dust that smeared their faces, the same dust that had burned their eyes and closed their throats all morning. It was the same dust that was churned up with every marching step. Now it was being churned up by the feet of American soldiers on the parched roads. The two enemy armies were about to meet each other.

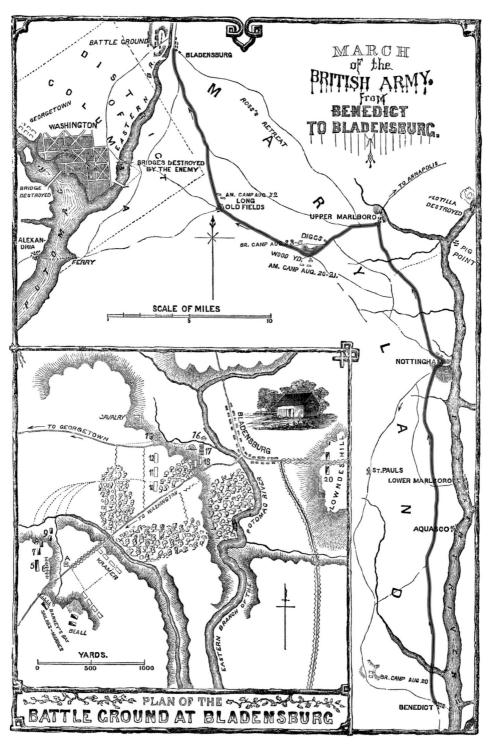

The advance of the British toward Washington is shown in red. The river near Bladensburg is the east branch of the Potomac, now called the Anacostia.

Chapter Four

Noon

What the Lady Saw

Dolley Madison continued her letter to her sister where she had left off the night before:

> Wednesday Morning, twelve o'clock.
>
> Since sunrise I have been turning my spy-glass in every direction, and watching with unwearied anxiety, hoping to discover the approach of my dear husband and his friends; but, alas! I can descry only groups of military, wandering in all directions, as if there was a lack of arms, or of spirit to fight for their own fireside.

She could only wonder what the day would bring to these soldiers, and to Washington.

A River Between Two Enemies

On the banks of the Potomac River, American militiamen waited for the British invaders. They had taken up position on the brow of a hill, drawn up in three lines. In front of the ranks, riflemen were stationed among the trees. To the right lay a dense wood. To the front and left was the river, which flowed between the men and the deserted town of Bladensburg. A narrow bridge connected the main street of the town to the bank on the other side, now thick with American soldiers.

The Fifth Regiment from Baltimore was at the front of the attack, ready to stand their ground. Among them was young Private Kennedy, wearing his "dashy" uniform and feathered helmet. Presumably he was still in the dress pumps he had tossed on the night before.

The Americans waited and watched, catching glimpses of scarlet as the enemy soldiers moved through the woods. The advancing British followed a sharp turn in the road. For a moment they were hidden by a screen of trees. Then, suddenly, there they were. The two armies looked at each other.

"We feel assured that the number and bravery of our men will afford complete protection to the city."
—*National Intelligencer,*
August 24, 1814

On his side of the river, young British officer George Gleig was impressed by the sheer number of American troops facing him and with their position on the hill. He thought that they numbered "nine thousand men, a number exactly doubling that of the force which was to attack them."

He was a good deal less impressed by the almost laughable appearance of the American militiamen. They were hardly the stern, well-ordered soldiers he was used to. As soon as they spotted the British, the Americans started hooting and hollering and filling the air with shouts. Though they were armed, most wore no uniforms. Some were dressed in black coats, others in blue, and still others in plain shooting jackets. Except for the fact that they were arranged in orderly lines, Gleig thought they might have passed for a crowd of spectators come to gawk at the British army. He noted mockingly:

> A few companies only, perhaps two, or at the most three battalions, wearing the blue jacket . . . presented some appearance of regular troops. The rest . . . seemed country people, who would have been much more appropriately employed in attending to their agricultural occupations, than in standing, with muskets in their hands, on the brow of a bare green hill.

The difference between the Americans and the column of British regulars, uniformed and disciplined, was stark:

> I have seldom been more forcibly struck with anything than with the contrast, which a glance to the rear afforded at this moment, with the spectacle which was before me. . . . The dress, the perfect regularity of their step, the good order which they preserved, and, above all, the internal conviction, that they were only advancing to victory, excited in me feelings for which I have no words.

Without a word, in perfect order, the British soldiers marched into the empty town. Each man steeled himself for what would come next.

First Shot

On the riverbank the Americans fired as the British advanced. With the first boom of cannon fire, three men fell. The guns were well placed, and the artillerymen were able to keep up a rapid and perfectly directed barrage on the streets of Bladensburg. Forced back, the invading soldiers scrambled to shield themselves behind houses. Still the American guns did not stop. One cannonball after another passed through the thin brick walls. Pinned down by the rain of cannon shot, Lieutenant Gleig saw a ball strike the young soldier lying next to him. It carried off the boy's leg.

On August 24, 1814, the bridge at Bladensburg became a bloody battleground.

Gleig knew there was only one way to advance. The British would have to cross the narrow bridge across the river and attack the American troops waiting on the riverbank. But he also knew that the bridge was completely exposed to American fire.

Then the order came. "The word was given to attack; and we immediately pushed on at double quick time, towards the head of the bridge." Taking it would only be accomplished with bloody consequences. It was a suicide mission.

Congreve rockets were aimed and launched from long poles, or "guide sticks." The whole system could be carried onto the battlefield easily (top) and set up quickly (bottom).

Chapter Five

Afternoon

The Devil's Artillery

A decade before the battle at Bladensburg, the British had begun work on a "secret weapon." Named for its developer, William Congreve, the Congreve rocket was not the first rocket designed for warfare. But it was an improvement on those that had come before. It also had advantages over the heavy cannons used at the time. The rocket was relatively inexpensive to make. It was also small, light, and portable. Where a cannon had to be hauled by a team of horses, a rocket could easily be carried by a single man on horseback. And because it was more stable to launch, it could be fired on the battlefield or from a ship.

But for all its advantages, the Congreve rocket was really more dramatic than deadly. It was almost impossible to aim accurately and

Top: Rockets being fired along the ground. This was especially effective against an attack by soldiers on horseback. Bottom: A town is bombarded by rockets before being invaded.

had an unfortunate habit of reversing course to attack its own launcher. Sometimes it fizzled without firing at all.

The real value of the rocket was as an instrument of terror. For people who had never experienced a weapon flying through the sky, the rocket seemed like something out of a nightmare. It hissed and smoked, trailing red fire behind it. It was almost impossible to evade as it flew low over the battlefield in wild twists and turns. Soldiers trying to run from it often found themselves meeting it head-on. The rocket excelled at spreading panic and confusion. One Russian general summed it up: "They look as if they were made in hell, and surely are the devil's own artillery."

Less than three weeks after the events of August 24, 1814, the British would use Congreve rockets in the attack on Fort McHenry in Baltimore. Lawyer and amateur poet Francis Scott Key would witness firsthand the rockets' red flames against the night sky—bright enough to illuminate the large American flag flying over the fort. He would be so moved by the sight of that flag still there at dawn that he would scribble a poem on the back of a letter. The poem, which came to be known as "The Star-Spangled Banner," would be set to music and in time become the national anthem of the United States. And Key's description of the Congreve rockets—"the rockets' red glare"—would become familiar to every American schoolchild.

Between noon and one o'clock on August 24, Dr. James Ewell was watching that red glare. He stood at the third-floor window of his home on Capitol Hill, just across the street from the Capitol itself. With him were his wife and daughters, trembling with fear. The family had been on edge all morning. News had been flying about the city since dawn that the enemy was approaching. The Ewells had seen the troops march out to Bladensburg to meet the British, and every moment they expected to hear the thunder of gunfire.

Standing at the window, they watched the Congreve rockets ascend over the treetops at Bladensburg. They heard the roar of the cannons. They knew that the battle had begun.

Blood on the Bridge

The bridge was narrow. No more than three men abreast could fit across at one time. The British swarmed onto it like ants.

Behind them men from the Royal Marine Artillery covered the assault with rocket fire. Some of the rockets arced over the American troops and headed toward the spot where James Madison and two of his advisers sat on horseback. Rockets began falling close to the president. The men decided it was time to move farther away.

On the hill above the bridge, the Americans waited. Then, when the bridge was covered with British soldiers, the cannons opened fire. The first shot mowed down nearly an entire company of regulars. American riflemen among the trees on the riverbank picked off others, forcing the survivors to fall back behind the houses again.

At this first success the Americans let out a deafening round of cheers. Lieutenant James Scott, Admiral Cockburn's aide-de-camp, overheard one wounded redcoat mocking the cheering, jeering Yankees across the river:

> A gallant soldier of the 85th, a Scotchman, whose arm had been shattered by a round-shot, and which was still dangling by a fibre to the stump, was seating himself on the steps of a house as the clamorous shout was rending the air: he coolly exclaimed, "Dinna halloo, my fine lads, you're no' yet out of the wood: wait a wee bit."

Within minutes the British had regrouped and made a fresh assault on the bridge. Once more the American guns roared. But this time the British did something the Americans clearly did not expect. They kept coming. According to Lieutenant Gleig, "'Forward, forward' was the only word heard." And forward they came, pressing on over the bridge in a single mass, trampling the dead and dying bodies of their comrades.

Baltimore volunteer Henry Fulford watched in awe as the British pushed forward despite the musket fire around them. "The fire I think, must have been dreadfully galling, but they took no notice of it; their men moved like clock-work; the instant a part of a platoon was cut down it was filled up by the men in the rear without the least noise and confusion whatever, so as to present always a solid column to the mouths of our cannon."

The untested militiamen at the front of the line had no idea what to make of this daring push. Unnerved, they made a very bad mistake. They stepped back. They fell back into the first line of infantry, throwing it into confusion before any of those soldiers had fired a shot. As the British charged forward, the American lines broke into disarray. Terrified soldiers began running for the woods. Lieutenant Gleig described the scene: "Our troops had scarcely shown themselves when the whole of that line gave way, and fled in the greatest confusion, leaving the two guns upon the road in possession of the victors."

The British soldiers in the front didn't wait for the rest of the army to catch up. Instead, they started chasing after the sprinting militiamen. The Americans were running so fast that the British had to toss aside their heavy knapsacks in order to keep up.

The remaining militiamen tried to stand their ground. Once more the cannons roared. Cannon shot pelted the rushing redcoats like hail and bit into the ground in deep furrows. The British were forced back all the way to the riverbank.

But this gave the other regulars time to cross the river and join the troops in the front. Stronger in number now, they pressed forward again, with the same result. One by one the remaining lines of militiamen faltered before the onslaught. These men began to run, too. One brave soldier tried to stop the mad rush by waving the flag he was carrying and marching forward a few steps. But the raw troops were too hard to rally. Before long there was nothing but a frenzied stampede toward the woods. According to Henry Fulford, "They were so strong that we had to give way. I think if we had remained ten minutes longer they would have either killed or taken the whole of us."

"Never did men with arms in their hands, make better use of their legs."
—Lieutenant George Gleig

Lieutenant Gleig had a different view: "The rout was now general throughout the line. The reserve, which ought to have supported the main body, fled as soon as those in front began to give way; and the cavalry, instead of charging the British troops, turned their horses' heads and galloped off."

Young Private Kennedy summed it up in his own way: "We made a fine scamper of it."

About two o'clock President Madison and his men were on their way back toward Washington. As they rode slowly along on horseback, a steady stream of militiamen began to pour past them. It was all too clear what had happened.

While the Cannons Roared

In 1814 twenty-eight thousand people lived in the District of Columbia, which included the city of Washington. Of those, eighteen hundred were slaves. Fifteen-year-old Paul Jennings was one of them. Paul had been born on James and Dolley Madison's estate, called Montpelier, in Orange, Virginia. The son of a female slave and an English trader, Paul grew to serve as James's valet, or personal servant.

Young Paul could read and write, which made him better educated than many poor white Americans of the day. As a valet he had a close-up view of the family, and he seems to have thought quite highly of them. Later in life he described the president as "one of the best men that ever lived. I never saw him in a passion, and never knew him to strike a slave, although he had over one hundred; neither would he allow an overseer to do it."

Dolley, he recalled, "was beloved by every body in Washington, white and colored. Whenever soldiers marched by, during the war,

Born a slave on the Madisons' estate, Paul Jennings moved with them to the White House when he was ten years old.

she always sent out and invited them in to take wine and refresh-
ments, giving them liberally of the best in the house."

Now, on August 24, he was one of only a few servants in the President's House with Dolley. The First Lady had spent the day watching
for her husband to arrive, by turns hopeful and despairing. For days
Paul had watched as people had filled the roads, fleeing Washington
in a panic. He had his own idea of the danger the city faced: "Every
thing seemed to be left to General Armstrong . . . who ridiculed the
idea that there was any danger. But, in August, 1814, the enemy had
got so near, there could be no doubt of their intentions." As if to
prove him right, the sound of cannon fire rumbled ominously from
the direction of Bladensburg, only four miles away.

But Paul had a job to do. The mid-afternoon meal at the White
House was served promptly at three o'clock every day, and Dolley
had decided that today would be no different. The table should be set
for forty. After the American army proved victorious, its commanders,
as well as the president's entire cabinet, were to be expected for lunch,
she told Paul. Whether she herself believed it was another matter.

Paul set the table himself. He went to the basement and brought
up ale, cider, and wine, which he placed in coolers in the dining room.
The cannons continued to boom.

While she waited for James, Dolley continued her letter to Lucy:
"Three o'clock. Will you believe it, my sister? we have had a battle,
or skirmish, near Bladensburg, and here I am still, within sound of
the cannon! Mr. Madison comes not. May God protect us!"

At about that time two messengers, covered in dust from the road,
arrived. Paul recognized one of them: "James Smith, a free colored man
who had accompanied Mr. Madison to Bladensburg, galloped up to
the house, waving his hat, and cried out 'Clear out, clear out! General

Armstrong has ordered a retreat!' "
The news caused a commotion among
those left in the White House. "All
then was confusion," Paul reported.

> "Oh how changed are my feelings,
> my confidence in our troops is gone."
> —Margaret Bayard Smith

The two messengers pleaded with
Dolley to flee the White House at once. The First Lady's response was
as calm as it was simple: "Here I mean to wait for him," she wrote Lucy.

A Tempting Target

On the battlefield the American commanders desperately tried to
stop the frantic retreat. One gave orders to his officers to cut down
any soldier who tried to run. No man was to leave his position, he
commanded. General Winder himself rode into the muddle, shout-
ing at his men to stand firm. But as soon as one group rallied,
another gave way. It quickly became clear that the officers' attempts
were futile. The battlefield was in chaos.

The rockets raining down only added to the confusion. They
hissed and twisted just above the heads of the men, blanketing the
field in a smoky haze. With no idea which way to run, the men scattered in every direction.

In the confusion Private Kennedy tried to help a friend and
ended up losing his gun:

> I lost my musket in the melee while bearing off a comrade,
> . . . whose leg was broken by a bullet. The day was very hot,
> and the weight of my wounded companion great, and not
> being able to carry both, I gave my musket to a friend who
> accompanied me, and he, afterwards being wounded himself,
> dropped his own weapon as well as mine.

Not more than one hundred forty yards from the militiamen, Admiral George Cockburn directed the aiming of the rockets. Seated on his white horse and wearing a hat and uniform trimmed in gleaming gold, he must have presented quite a striking sight. His aide, Lieutenant Scott, worried that he also made a tempting target. He was in full sight of the enemy, and Scott begged him to move to safety behind some rocks by the side of the road. He reminded Cockburn that the Americans would surely see his death as a great victory.

The admiral scoffed at the suggestion.

> "Poh! poh! nonsense!" was the only reply, whilst he was eagerly watching a couple of rockets that were on the point of being discharged. . . . The fiery missiles went directly into the enemy's ranks, creating a fearful gap, and a much more fearful panic in the immediate vicinity—"Capital!" he exclaimed, "excellent!"

Suddenly a musket ball zinged toward the admiral. It passed between his leg and the flap of his saddle, cutting the leather of his stirrup in two. But by some miracle, both Admiral Cockburn and his horse were untouched.

"Board 'Em!"

Not every American on the battlefield that afternoon was an untested militiaman. Commodore Joshua Barney was a hero of the Revolutionary War. Now in his mid-fifties, he could have been enjoying a comfortable retirement on his farm. Instead, in 1813, as British ships were terrorizing towns along the coast, he had contacted Secretary of the Navy William Jones with a bold plan.

Barney called for the construction of a fleet of small barges that could be rowed easily in shallow water. The barges could be quickly and cheaply built. Each would be armed with one cannon and serve as a crude gunboat.

By May 1814 his flotilla of eighteen barges was ready. All that summer Barney's flotilla acted as a "mosquito fleet," darting in to attack larger British ships before retreating to one shallow creek or another for safety. He had no hope of sinking any of the heavier ships. His aim was simply to keep them busy. The plan worked. Because of Barney and his men, the "monster" Cockburn's attacks of the previous summer were not repeated.

By late August, as the British prepared to invade Washington, they had had quite enough of the pesky Commodore Barney. British

Joshua Barney commanded his first ship at age fourteen, when his captain died suddenly at sea. On August 24, 1814, he was fifty-five years old and an experienced naval officer.

ships pursued the flotilla up the Patuxent River, bottling it up. On the morning of August 22, the British approached and made ready to seize the American boats. Suddenly the barges, one after another, blew up in their stunned faces. Within minutes the flotilla was sunk in the mud. Barney and his men had sacrificed their mosquito fleet and fled inland, dragging five of their cannons behind them.

Now, on the afternoon of August 24, they took their place on the battlefield. They had not been ordered to Bladensburg until the last minute, so they arrived after the battle had begun. Already the lines of American militiamen were beginning to crumble around them. Barney set up his five guns on a hillside overlooking a road and waited. When the enemy appeared below, he blasted away, sweeping the road clear. Twice more the attempt was made. Twice more, Barney's guns roared and drove the enemy back.

The British tried a new direction, advancing to Barney's right. He ordered his sailors and marines to attack while he directed the cannon fire. His men charged down the hill, the sailors bellowing their war cry: "Board 'em!" In a fury of gunfire and bayonets, the British were pushed back yet again.

But by this time nearly all the other American troops had fled in a panic. In the confusion the wagon with all their ammunition had disappeared as well. Barney and his five hundred men had been left to face the enemy alone.

Suddenly a British bullet struck Barney's horse, killing it. Moments later Barney himself was seriously wounded by a musket ball in the thigh. The men were running out of ammunition. Still they battled on, fighting the enemy hand to hand. As the British advanced on his position, Barney knew there was no hope. He ordered his men to leave him and retreat while they could.

The British were amazed at the dogged courage of Barney and his men. Even Lieutenant Gleig could not help expressing his admiration:

> Of the sailors, however, it would be injustice not to speak in the terms which their conduct merits. They were employed as gunners, and not only did they serve their guns with a quickness and precision which astonished their assailants, but they stood till some of them were actually bayoneted, with fuzes in their hands; nor was it till their leader was wounded and taken, and they saw themselves deserted on all sides by the soldiers, that they quitted the field.

Perhaps the highest praise came from Admiral Cockburn: "They have given us the only fighting we have had."

The admiral, who knew a great man when he saw one, expressed genuine concern when he was led to the wounded Barney. He waited with him as an English surgeon tended to his wounds. Then, to Barney's shock, he set the American free.

What It Means When the Cannons Stop

In Washington the Ewell family had spent the afternoon at their third-floor window. They had been able to trace the progress of the battle by the arc of the rockets and the thunder of the guns. Suddenly, toward late afternoon, the cannons fell silent. Dr. Ewell could only wonder what it meant. His feelings chased each other: first hopeful that his country had prevailed, then fearing that all was lost. The suspense did not last long: "I soon discovered the dust beginning to rise above the forests in thick clouds, on whose dark tops, growing larger and larger every minute and rapidly advancing, I read the dismal fate that awaited us."

On the streets below he saw a horrifying sight: "crowds of gentlemen on horse-back, some of whom loudly bawled out as they came on, 'Fly, fly! the ruffians are at hand! If you cannot get away yourselves, for God's sake send off your wives and daughters, for the ruffians are at hand!'" Behind them came a long line of infantry and cavalry. They were moving so fast they churned up thick clouds of dust. To Dr. Ewell it seemed as if nature itself were in motion.

> "The raw militiamen . . . fled like frightened sheep in every direction, except, indeed, towards the enemy."
> —Dr. James Ewell

Leading the pack, in full flight, was the unfortunate secretary of war, John Armstrong. Presumably he was at last convinced that Washington was indeed in danger.

Saving George Washington

Somehow at this late hour, Dolley Madison managed to find a cart. Into it she packed most of the White House silver, some papers, books, and a small clock. She also tucked in her prized red velvet curtains from the oval drawing room, the only memento of her famous "Wednesdays." But everything else—clothes, family keepsakes, even her letters from James—would have to be left behind.

People continued to stream to the President's House, urging her to flee. By now she was beginning to understand that it was too dangerous for her to wait for her husband. But still she would not be hurried. She had one last task to undertake, and to her it seemed a very important one. She explained to Lucy: "Our kind friend, Mr. Carroll, has come to hasten my departure, and [is] in a very bad humor with me, because I insist on waiting until the large picture of General Washington is secured, and it requires to be unscrewed from the wall."

The picture was the magnificent state portrait of the first president that hung in the dining room. To Dolley it was unthinkable that it should be left behind. At best, it would be burned along with the rest of the house and its contents. At worst, it would become a prize of war to be insulted by rough soldiers. Either possibility was unbearable.

But unscrewing the full-length painting from the wall was no simple matter. Dolley had Paul Jennings and another servant working on it, but time was growing perilously short. When a family friend from New York arrived with another man, Dolley made a decision. She called for an ax. "I have ordered the frame to be broken, and the canvas taken out. It is done! and the precious portrait placed in the hands of two gentlemen of New York, for safe keeping."

It was time for her to leave. She told a friend later that in spite of the awful threats against her, what she felt was defiance. "I confess that I was so unfeminine as to be free from fear, and willing to remain in the Castle! If I could have had a cannon through every window . . ."

She concluded her letter to her sister, begun the evening before: "And now, dear sister, I must leave this house, or the retreating army will make me a prisoner in it by filling up the road I am directed to take. When I shall again write to you, or where I shall be tomorrow, I cannot tell!"

On her way to the door, she scooped up whatever silver would fit into a little bag. Then she left the house and climbed into the carriage with her maid and the fuming Mr. Carroll, headed to his home in Georgetown. She would never live in the White House again.

The servants left, too, one with a feather bed lashed to his carriage. Another rescued Polly the macaw and carried her in her cage to a neighboring house for safekeeping.

Thanks to Dolley Madison, the Gilbert Stuart portrait of George Washington still hangs in the White House today.

After all Dolley's fretful hours of waiting, she had not waited quite long enough. Less than an hour later, James arrived to find her gone. He stayed only a short while, to get something to eat and drink and to send his wife a message to meet him in Virginia. Then he, too, was gone.

That did not end the parade of visitors to the President's House, however. Teenage slave Paul Jennings had gone to a neighboring stable to fetch a horse and carriage when he chanced to look back. He was dismayed at the scene: "A rabble, taking advantage of the confusion, ran all over the White House, and stole lots of silver and whatever they could lay their hands on."

Afternoon at the Races

By four in the afternoon, the battle was over. Few militiamen lost their lives in the retreat. They were simply running too fast for the British soldiers to catch up. Before long, people were calling the battle "the Bladensburg Races."

In his official report Admiral Cockburn boasted that the attack was "crowned with the Success it merited." He even joked that they had captured a few prisoners, "tho' not many, owing to the Swiftness with which the Enemy went off."

The British did not press on right away. Those who were uninjured were exhausted by the rapid march and the heat. A dozen men had already dropped dead not of wounds but of heatstroke. General Ross had no choice but to order a rest.

They would wait for the cool of evening to invade Washington. There was nothing more standing in their way.

> "The red coats got a little the better of you at the start, but you beat them *in the long run.*"
> —Taunt directed at a member of the militia who had been at "the Bladensburg Races"

A view of Pennsylvania Avenue from the Capitol. Pierre L'Enfant's "grand avenue" extended from the Capitol to the President's House.

Chapter Six

Dusk

Wilderness City

In 1789, when the new nation decided it needed a new capital city, Pierre L'Enfant stepped up to the task. The French engineer wrote to President George Washington and offered his services. In 1791 he arrived at the city-to-be, full of enthusiasm and ideas.

L'Enfant was clearly brimming with imagination. Where others saw woods and swamps, he saw a city on a grand, almost majestic, scale. His plan called for monumental buildings, statues, columns, and no fewer than five gushing fountains. The streets were to be broad enough for several lanes of traffic. He proposed an enormous presidential "palace," five times bigger than the house that was eventually built. His new capital city would be something between ancient Rome and a European royal court.

Unfortunately, the haughty L'Enfant turned out to be difficult to work with. After he was fired, the flashier parts of his plan were scaled back. The "President's Palace" became the "President's House."

But his plan for the city had a supporter in George Washington. L'Enfant had given the city room to grow. The president liked the idea of a place that met present-day needs as well as those of future generations. It was a city planned "for ages to come."

In 1814 that age had not yet arrived. Washington was a city that had been forced out of a wilderness of forests, fields, and swamps, and the ghosts of its former self were everywhere. L'Enfant's broad avenues were mostly still just dirt roads. They were dusty in summer, muddy in winter, and nearly always rutted and hard to travel. Pedestrians tripped over tree stumps. And the only creatures happy about all those swamps were the mosquitoes. Most anyone who could afford to leave the city did so during the buggy summer months.

The tourist Miss Brown, who had so admired Dolley Madison on the Fourth of July, was less happy with the city itself: "Passing over a mile of rough road, bordered here and there by Congress boarding-houses, with veritable swamps between, you came to the President's house—beautiful with architecture, upholstery, gilding and paintings, set down in the midst of rough, unornamented grounds."

"We frequented the parties, the dinners, the assemblies . . . almost at the risk of life . . . the city not being laid out, the streets not graduated, the bridges consisting of mere loose planks, and huge stumps of trees recently cut down intercepting every path."
—Louisa Adams, wife of John Quincy Adams

"[Washington was] a meagre village, a place with a few bad houses and extensive swamps."
—Attorney General Richard Rush

George Washington had hoped that the new city would be thriving by 1800, the year the government officially moved there. But fourteen years later, there were still only about ten thousand people who called Washington home. There were two thousand houses, and those were scattered far apart, three or four to a street. People used mocking nicknames such as "Wilderness City," "City of Magnificent Distances," or "City of Streets Without Houses."

It was no small wonder that the secretary of war had looked around and wondered aloud why the British would bother to invade such a place. The flourishing port city of Baltimore, only forty-five miles away, was surely a more attractive target.

But Washington had something that Baltimore did not. It had the Washington Navy Yard.

Located on the eastern branch of the Potomac (now called the Anacostia River), the Washington Navy Yard had been planned even before the government moved to Washington. It was the pride of the young nation's navy and of the city itself. The yard was where the country's warships were built, launched, supplied, and maintained. It was a vital link between the United States Navy and its ships at sea—the ships now in combat with British warships.

That made the Navy Yard a valuable prize of war indeed. Even had Washington not been the capital, the Navy Yard made the city a tempting target to the invading British.

A City Silent as a Church

Mordecai Booth knew a terrible secret.

Booth was a clerk at the Washington Navy Yard. On Wednesday, August 24, he had gone home for his dinner and had just finished when news arrived of the American retreat. The city was already in chaos: "Waggons and Men . . . were seen flying in the utmost confusion." He rushed back to work to do whatever he could.

He found Commodore Thomas Tingey, head of the Navy Yard. Tingey had overseen the building of the yard and had been its commandant since its founding in 1799. The yard was his baby. He was nearly alone there now. Most of the workmen, sailors, and marines who would have been at the yard on a normal workday had left to join the fighting. Still others had fled in the panic.

Booth offered Tingey his assistance. It was then that he heard the awful word: Tingey confided that in the event of a retreat or a defeat, he had been ordered by Secretary Jones himself to burn the Navy Yard to the ground. It was the only way to keep American ships and equipment from falling into enemy hands. And as he was so shorthanded, he asked Booth to help him light the fires.

Booth was stunned. It was hard enough to believe that the city might fall to the British, but the prospect of having to torch the Navy Yard was unthinkable. Booth had a proposition. He had a particularly good horse already saddled and ready, he told Tingey. Why not use it to scout the city and find out for sure what had happened? He would see whether all really was lost or if their soldiers might still make a stand and save the city.

Tingey, who was no more eager than Booth to see the yard in flames, agreed. He would put off firing the yard until the last possible moment. As Booth mounted his horse and rode off, he thought he heard the sound of cannonballs whistling through the air.

On the road Booth had a good view of the hills beyond. He had expected to see the British army advancing toward the city. What he saw instead appalled him. "I saw not the Appearance of an Englishman—But Oh! my Country— . . . I saw the Commons Covered with the fugitive Soldiery of our Army—runing, hobling, Creaping, & appearently pannick struck."

> "No time was lost, in making the necessary arrangements, for firing the whole, and preparing boats for departing from the yard."
> —Commodore Thomas Tingey

He managed to find some hope in the dismal scene, since at least there were no British soldiers in sight. One of the militiamen told him that the army was to rally at the Capitol building. Booth urged his horse on toward the Capitol. But there he found only men resting from the heat and the battle—mostly Commodore Barney's flotilla men. There was no officer above the rank of captain to lead them, and the two captains he did find were arguing over who should command.

As he rode about the city, he was struck by the scene: "I saw Officers, as well as men at their doors." It appeared to Booth as if most of the militiamen had simply taken refuge in their own homes after the retreat. Someone told him that the army had gone on to the heights of Georgetown, but he could not believe that. Surely the militia would not have left the capital city unprotected.

Eventually Booth realized that if he wanted to know anything for sure, he was going to have to find a more reliable source of information. He turned his "good horse" toward the President's House—"by which I might assertain by some one to be relied on, what was the fact, and if any thing was to be done."

One lone colonel on horseback guarded the White House, and the situation apparently had the man on edge. When Booth asked for his name, "He Seem'd much Agitated, was About to draw a pistol from his holster— . . . I perceived he was an American as well as myself, and requesting him, not to be flurried—that my object was to gain correct information of our Army; he informed me his Name was Tatum . . . and he returned his Pistol."

Colonel Tatum informed Booth that no one was inside—he himself had called for John, the White House butler, and had gotten no answer. Still, he tried again: "[He] Dismounted—went up the steps, pulled the Bell several times with much violence—Knocked at the Door, and called John—But all was as silent as a Church."

The President's House was deserted.

Booth suddenly understood that the worst had happened: "Then, and not untill then, was my mind fully impressed that, the Matropelis of our Country was abandoned to it's horrid fate."

As the sun began to set, Booth continued to scout the city. Along the way he was joined by several other men. At Capitol Hill they saw not one soul. The group had nearly reached Long's Hotel, where James Madison's inaugural ball had been held in happier times, when one of the men thought he saw something in the fading light. He leaned forward over his horse's neck, straining for a better look. Booth thought the shapes in the distance looked like cows, and he said so. Yes, agreed the man, he saw the cows—but he also thought he saw men.

The scouts pressed their horses forward until they were no more than forty yards from the dim figures. Suddenly they realized they were looking at a party of men advancing straight toward them. British soldiers! The group wheeled their horses around, but not before they were spotted and fired on by the enemy.

Booth realized that the dreaded time had come. He hurried his horse to the Navy Yard to make his report.

By the Light of the Setting Sun

The capital resembled a ghost town. Shops were closed. Office doors were locked. Residents who had not taken the opportunity to flee remained housebound. The curious peered out from behind curtains or from half-open doorways.

The normally bustling streets were strangely quiet now. In the heavy late-August air, the approaching tread of many booted feet could clearly be heard.

Nine-year-old slave Michael Shiner was one of the few out on the street. He was standing with two others on Capitol Hill when he spotted the enemy heading toward the city. The sun was now sinking low over the horizon. Its final rays lit up the advancing troops like a flame. Many years later, the memory of that sight was still sharp: "As son [soon] as we got a sight of British armmy raising that hill they looked like flames of fier all red coats and the stoks of ther guns painted with red ver Milon [vermillion] and the iron work shind like a spanish dollar."

The invasion of Washington had begun.

The Washington Navy Yard, restored after the fire.

Chapter Seven

Night

The Fuse Is Lit

It was after dark when Mordecai Booth arrived at the Navy Yard. Another of the scouts, Captain John Creighton, came with him. Commodore Thomas Tingey was waiting anxiously. He had set himself a deadline of eight thirty. If the scouts had not returned by then, he would assume that they had been captured. He would have to torch the yard himself.

Booth reported to Tingey what he had seen: the British had indeed arrived in Washington. The men knew what they had to do. Even at this late stage, Creighton tried to stop them, protesting that he could not bear to destroy the yard. Tingey, who no doubt felt the same way, reminded him that Secretary Jones's orders were clear. They had a duty to do, and there would be no further discussion. The first of the blazes set that night would be set by the Americans themselves.

They lit the fires. Wooden storehouses and sheds burned quickly. Sailcloth, rope, and piles of lumber for shipbuilding added fuel to the flames. Within moments the blaze was so intense the men could not have stopped it if they had wanted to.

At the wharf, two new warships, the frigate *Columbia* and the sloop *Argus*, were nearly completed and ready to be launched. The ships represented the finest craftsmanship of the yard's skilled workmen. In short order they were torched, too.

With the fires burning, the men turned to their escape. Tingey and Creighton decided they would cross the river by rowboat. But Booth still had his "good horse" with him and did not want to turn it loose. He would rely on his horse to get him safely out of the city.

The flames from the burning Navy Yard lit up the night sky.

It was time to say good-bye. Tingey told Booth to take care of himself and his horse. Then, perhaps remembering the eight-thirty deadline he had set for himself, he pulled out his watch and re-marked casually on the time. It was twenty minutes after eight.

Booth hurried his horse away from the burning Navy Yard: "I passed from the Yard . . . to the Potomac Bridge—The South draw [bridge] was up—I had it put down—and was scarcely over, before I saw the flames of the Yard." They were shooting toward the sky.

Just moments later, as he galloped on, he heard a deafening boom. He could only imagine it was the Navy Yard's ammunitions supply exploding as the yard burned to the ground.

Washington in Enemy Hands

General Ross and Admiral Cockburn entered Washington to the long, loud roll of a drum, the signal that they were ready to discuss the terms of the capital's surrender. They were prepared to be generous, so long as the city surrendered peacefully, and they were a little miffed when no one seemed to be paying much attention. In truth, there were few people left in the city they had just invaded. The president and his cabinet had escaped and the militiamen had fled, as had most of the residents. Those who were left gave quick evidence of what they thought of the enemy's generous offer.

The British had just reached the open space in front of the Capitol when a volley of gunshots sounded from a house on their right. General

> "Admiral Cockburn would have burnt the whole {city}, but Ross would only consent to the burning of the public buildings."
>
> —Captain Harry Smith

Ross's horse fell dead on the spot. One of the British guards was killed as well, and another wounded.

The British were furious. They had been prepared to spare private homes from destruction, but as this one had been used for an ambush, it was now fair game.

Nine-year-old Michael Shiner, who had continued to watch as the British entered the city, described what happened next:

> In a twinkale of the eye house Wher sorouned [surrounded] By British armmy and search all through up stairs and down stairs in search of the Man that shot the horse from under genral but no Man was found after they found that they couldent find the Man they put a slow Match to the house and then stood off a sertin ditance and forong [firing?] those congreve Rocket those Rocket burnt until the[y] came to the explosion part they Made the rafters fly east and West.

Having taken their revenge on the offending house, the British turned their attention to the Capitol. By now, the glow from the blazing Navy Yard twelve blocks to the south had turned the night as bright as day. So the invaders had no trouble seeing the magnificent structure in front of them. It was their first glimpse of the symbol of Yankee authority, now captured in the name of the Crown.

The Capitol was more like two buildings connected by a long, unpainted wooden shed. The north wing was used by the Senate, the south by the House of Representatives. Though still unfinished, it was an imposing sight. Lieutenant Gleig, who was altogether unimpressed by the other buildings in Washington, was impressed by this one. He described the Capitol as "an edifice of some beauty. . . . It was built entirely of freestone, tastefully worked and highly polished;

and, besides its numerous windows, was lighted from the top by a large and handsome cupola. . . . Its central appearance was light, airy, and elegant."

The soldiers broke in through the enormous doors at the east entrance. Once inside they were stunned by what they saw. Instead of crude Yankee workmanship, they beheld elegance and refined beauty. Lieutenant Scott, who had accompanied Admiral Cockburn inside, was particularly taken with the chamber before him:

> Each of the senators and representatives had a handsome desk appropriated to his use, arranged in a semicircular order around the presidential chair [actually the Speaker's chair], over which was placed a handsome clock, surmounted by a gilt eagle with extended wings and ruffled crest, looking towards the skies, emblematical, it is to be presumed, of the rising greatness of the young nation.

A wing of the Capitol before August 24, 1814.

The chamber was surrounded by striking, intricately carved columns. Between the columns hung fine silk curtains in a rich crimson color. Scott thought the splendor of the room more suited for a king than for elected officials.

But the British had not come to gawk like common tourists. Admiral Cockburn got them back on track. According to one story, he mocked the purpose of the room, mounting the Speaker's chair and bellowing: "Shall this harbor of Yankee democracy be burned? All for it will say aye." At the roar of agreement, he pronounced the vote unanimous. The soldiers set to work.

First they tried to ignite the building by firing rockets through the roof. When it refused to catch, they made a bonfire of the mahogany tables and chairs in the chamber. Soon everything in the room that could catch fire was swallowed in the blaze. Ribbons of flame chased each other along the elegant drapery. In the fierce heat the columns cracked and buckled. The lovely carvings crumbled to the floor.

As he left the room, Lieutenant Scott noticed the eagle he had so admired: "Its funereal pile was lighted up as the clock under it told the hour of ten."

Quickly the invaders moved from room to room, setting fire to each. In an office used by James Madison, Admiral Cockburn pocketed a slim book stamped "President of the U. States." It was an odd souvenir. The book itself was only a list of government payments, and of little consequence. But the admiral was so pleased with his clever theft that he later presented the book to his brother, inscribed: "Taken in President's Room in the Capitol, at the destruction of that building by the British, on the Capture of Washington 24th. August 1814 by Admiral Cockburn—& by him presented to his Eldest Brother Sir

James Cockburn of Langton Bart Governor of Bermuda."

Not all the British were as proud of their actions that night. Years later Captain Harry Smith wrote with regret: "I had no objection to burn arsenals, dockyards, frigates building, stores, barracks, etc., but . . . we were horrified at the order to burn the elegant Houses of Parliament and the President's house."

> "A noble library, several printing offices, and all the national archives were likewise committed to the flames, which, though no doubt the property of Government, might better have been spared."
> —Lieutenant George Gleig

Some were especially bothered by the destruction of the Library of Congress, located inside the Capitol. Occupying the western half of the Senate wing, the library had only a wooden shingled roof above it. It burned like kindling. Every one of its three thousand books was reduced to ashes.

Dr. Ewell, who had watched the rockets fly over the battlefield at Bladensburg—and seen the secretary of war hotfooting it away from the action—had moved with his family to the house of a neighbor, hoping it might be safer there. He was only a few doors down from the Capitol when it burned. "Never shall I forget my tortured feelings when I beheld that noble edifice wrapt in flames, which, bursting through the windows and mounting far above its summits, with a noise like thunder, filled all the saddened night with a dismal gloom."

Around ten thirty, their work done, Admiral Cockburn and General Ross left Capitol Hill with about one hundred fifty men. In two columns they marched down stately, tree-lined Pennsylvania Avenue toward the President's House. Behind them the Capitol was an inferno. Set on a hill as L'Enfant had envisioned it, it burned like a beacon to the entire city.

Uninvited Guests

It had been a week to rattle anyone's nerves. Washington resident Barbara Suter called it "a whole week of great trouble, hardly sleeping at night, and all the day time spent in fright."

The elderly widow ran a boardinghouse on a corner of Pennsylvania Avenue, not far from the President's House. She had already had one encounter with a British soldier. Just a few days earlier, a man claiming to be a British deserter had appeared at her door. He

The Capitol after the fire. The damage from the flames and smoke is clearly visible.

was dressed in shabby clothes and begged her for something to eat. One of her boarders protested. The man might be an imposter—or worse, a spy—he warned. But Mrs. Suter was too kindhearted to turn the hungry man away.

Now her boarders were gone. The nervous lady found herself alone in the house with only a woman servant. As the Capitol burned and explosions from the Navy Yard rocked the night, soldiers surrounded her long, low brick house.

At first she took the uniformed men in the shadows for American

militiamen. Of course, that was wishful thinking. Her worst fear was realized when a British officer strode into the house. He announced himself as General Ross and ordered the terrified Mrs. Suter to prepare a supper for him and his officers. The poor woman tried excuses: she had no food in the house and besides, there was McLeod's Tavern across the way, which might better suit him.

But the general insisted. It was not so much the food he wanted but the view, he told her. He preferred her home, with its view of the public buildings. Then, teasingly, he told her he already knew all about her. To prove it, he asked about her boarder who had objected to giving food to a poor British soldier in distress.

Then Mrs. Suter remembered the deserter. She realized to her horror that she had been tricked. She had indeed aided a British spy.

The general warned her to have supper ready when he and his officers returned. After he left, the frightened woman went into the yard to chase chickens in the dark. She would have to hurry to get a chicken dinner on the table for her uninvited guests.

The White House Is Burning

The crunch of booted feet on the gravel of Pennsylvania Avenue had stopped. The remaining residents of Washington waited to hear the roar and crackle of flames that would signal the destruction of the White House, the symbol of the president himself.

But the British were taking their time. As they had with the Capitol, they wanted to poke around a bit first. The violation of the home of the president of the United States was something to be savored.

In the dining room they found the broken frame that had held the portrait of George Washington. The pieces were still screwed to the wall, and the soldiers must have wondered what had hung there. But they paid more attention to the elaborate table set by Paul Jennings hours earlier. Lieutenant Gleig could only assume that the feast had been prepared for returning American military leaders. Clearly there would be no such victory banquet.

> Instead of being devoured by American officers, it went to satisfy the less delicate appetites of a party of English soldiers. . . . Several kinds of wine in handsome cut-glass decanters were cooling on the sideboard; . . . whilst in the kitchen . . . spits, loaded with joints [of meat] of various sorts, turned before the fire; pots, saucepans, and other culinary utensils, stood upon the grate.

The hungry, thirsty men helped themselves to food and drink. In a jollier mood they helped themselves to souvenirs, too. A parcel of notes President Madison had written to his wife, a small medicine chest, the president's fine dress sword—all became loot.

Some of the soldiers voiced disappointment that they had not been able to capture the Madisons. So they made do. One man found a hat belonging to James and hoisted it up on the tip of his bayonet. If they could not capture "the little president," he said, at least they could parade his hat in London. From Dolley's parlor someone snatched a small portrait of her, saying he would "keep Dolley safe and exhibit her in London."

As he had at the Capitol, Admiral Cockburn took center stage. He pulled an American bystander from the street and forced the poor man to take part in the evening's fun. The man, a young bookseller named Roger Chew Weightman, happened to be a friend of Margaret Smith's. She later reported what the young man told her.

[Cockburn] insisted on young Weightman's sitting down and drinking Jemmy's health, which was the only epithet he used whenever he spoke of the President. After looking round, he told Mr. W. to take something to remember this day. Mr. W. wished for some valuable article. No, no said he, *that* I must give to the flames, but here, handing him some ornaments off the mantle-piece, these will answer as a memento. I must take something too.

Cockburn chose an old hat of "Jemmy's" and a cushion from Dolley's chair as his trophies. He added a coarse joke, saying that the cushion would remind him of Mrs. Madison's "seat."

Lieutenant Scott had a good look around the house, too. "Passing through the President's dressing-room . . . , the snowy clean linen tempted me to take the liberty of making a very fair exchange; I accordingly doffed my inner garment, and thrust my unworthy person into a shirt belonging to no less a personage than the chief magistrate of the United States."

Soon enough it was time to get down to business. Dolley's fine furniture was tossed into heaps. Curtains were yanked down. Lamp oil was poured onto bedding. Then fifty men surrounded the house. Anna Maria Thornton watched from the heights of nearby Georgetown and told her friend Margaret Smith of the horrifying scene:

Each [carried] a long pole to which was fixed a ball about the circumference of a large plate,—when arrived at the building, each man was station'd at a window, with his pole and machine of wild-fire against it, at the word of command, at the same instant the windows were broken and this wild-fire thrown in, so that an instantaneous conflagration took place and the whole building was wrapt in flames and smoke. The spectators stood in awful silence, the city was light and the heavens redden'd with the blaze!

The floors and walls of the house were of wood, and the arsonists had done their job well. Captain Harry Smith boasted, "Our sailors were artists at the work." The fires burned so hot that metal lightning rods on the roof warped and twisted like snakes. Soon there was nothing left of Dolley's elegant rooms but ash, soot, and memories.

The soldiers' work was not yet over. When they were finished with the White House, they left to put the torch to the Treasury Building, too.

Dining by Firelight

Barbara Suter was busy preparing for her British "guests." But she could not possibly have missed the goings-on just down the street. As she worked, her house was bathed in the warm glow of firelight from the blazing buildings nearby.

As he had promised, General Ross arrived with ten of his officers, ready for dinner. Admiral Cockburn preferred to make his own entrance. For added insult he tried to ride into the house on a mule, but he only got partway through the low front door. He hopped off and introduced himself to the shocked woman as the Admiral Cockburn she had no doubt heard so much about.

At the table he immediately blew out the candles she had lit. He preferred to dine by the light of the burning President's House and Treasury Building, he told her playfully. The flames were bright enough to light up the whole room.

Mrs. Suter had two sons in the military, one of whom had fought alongside Commodore Barney that afternoon and been wounded. Now she was forced to wait on enemy soldiers and listen to their mealtime chitchat. They had been looking forward to showing off James and Dolley in England, they said, and were bitterly disappointed that the two had escaped. Every man had his own theory as to where they might be hiding.

The cracked, blackened shell of the White House after the fire. A lightning rod, melted into an S, is at top.

While they were still eating, another officer came in and suggested that they still had the War Office to burn. Admiral Cockburn was all for it. General Ross vetoed the idea for the time being: "It will be time enough in the morning, as it is now growing late, and the men require rest."

When the meal was finished, the men left, without even a tip of the hat to thank the woman who had provided it. As they left,

Mrs. Suter realized that she recognized two of them. One she had seen often in the city before the war. The other was the spy who'd been at her door earlier in the week. She had just fed him for the second time.

My Country, 'Tis of Thee . . .

In a world without electricity, the fires were the brightest light in the night for miles around. The flames were visible forty-five miles away in Baltimore. They outshone even the moon.

"You never saw a drawing room so brilliantly lighted as the whole city was that night," one woman wrote. "Few thought of going to bed—they spent the night in gazing on the fires and lamenting the disgrace of the city."

The pull of the scene was irresistible. All night, people could not tear themselves from the sight. They watched with noses pressed to windows, or from hillsides, or from woods or cornfields where they'd fled to hide.

Dolley Madison had made it to a friend's home in Virginia, about ten miles from Washington. Though she'd been up since dawn, sleep was out of the question. She spent the night at the window, watching her home and her city burn.

James Madison saw the fires from horseback as he rode through the countryside, hoping to get back to Washington as soon as it was safe. From time to time he lost sight of the flames, but at each hilltop they reappeared, and he paused to watch. Attorney General Richard Rush was with him and described the scene: "I have . . . the vivid impression upon my eye of columns of flame and smoke ascending throughout the night of the 24th of August from the Capitol,

President's house, and other public edifices, as the whole were on fire, some burning slowly, others with bursts of flame and sparks mounting high up in the dark horizon."

Paul Jennings had sought refuge in the home of a Methodist minister. "In the evening, while he was at prayer, I heard a tremendous explosion, and, rushing out, saw that the public buildings, navy yard, ropewalks, &c., were on fire."

On Capitol Hill Dr. Ewell had continued to watch from his neighbor's house as, one by one, the beautiful public buildings were destroyed. "The conflagration of these noble and splendid buildings spread a glare over the night that was truly awful."

Teenage tourist Miss Brown had escaped the city. She spent the night camping on the shore of the Potomac with a number of other families and children, waiting for makeshift boats to take them to safety. It would have been a merry scene, except that every so often they kept turning to gaze at the "large portion of the horizon illuminated by the burning Capitol and other public buildings."

Navy Yard clerk Mordecai Booth saw the flames from a hilltop after crossing the Potomac into Virginia. A crowd of others, mostly women and children, joined him to watch. For nearly three hours Booth stood there, unable to tear himself away. The sight—"A sight, so repugnant to my feelings, so dishonourable; so degrading to the American Character, and at the Same time, so Awful"— left him practically weak with grief.

One man who did not see the fires was State Department clerk Stephen Pleasonton. He had ridden thirty-five miles, carrying the Declaration

"At first I thought the world must be on fire—such a flame I have never seen since. We were told the British had taken Washington and {were} burning it up.... I was told not to cry."
—seven-year-old Matilda Roberts, Baltimore

of Independence, the Constitution, and other irreplaceable documents in his homemade linen sacks. He had finally found a safe place in Virginia to hide the ordinary-looking bags with their extraordinary cargo, but the long ride and the stress of the job had worn him out. He found a hotel, went right to bed, and slept through the whole invasion. He had to be told about the fires the next morning.

While he slept, a storm blew into Washington. Winds fanned the flames of the burning buildings. At the White House, floors, ceilings,

British forces capture the city of Washington, seen enveloped in smoke and flames on a hill. The burning ships of the Navy Yard are at left.

and inner walls came crashing down, leaving only the outer shell. Sudden cold rain sizzled on the heated stone walls, cracking them. The Capitol was much the same: blackened stone surrounding a charred ruin.

But thirty-five miles away, in plain cloth sacks in an empty house in Leesburg, Virginia, the Declaration of Independence and the Constitution were safe. The most sacred documents of the nation would survive the invasion.

Americans were incensed when they heard of Admiral Cockburn's behavior in the Capitol.

Chapter Eight

The Day After

Solemn Morning

Margaret Smith, who had fled Washington in the predawn dark, had found safety for her family in the peaceful little village of Brookeville, Maryland. But there was no outrunning the news that was everywhere.

"Thursday morning. This morning on awakening we were greeted with the sad news, that our city was taken, the bridges and public buildings burnt, our troops flying in every direction. Our little army totally dispersed. Good God, what will be the event!"

"The state of our country, has wrung tears of anguish from me."
—Margaret Bayard Smith

A Monster's Revenge

The acrid smell of smoke hung over an occupied Washington. For the invaders, morning meant a return to the activities of the previous night. There was more to burn.

First up were the State and War Departments. The ever-thorough British would have burned the Patent Office, too, but the head of the office convinced them it would be a shame to burn patent models and drawings that might be of use to all. It was let alone.

Admiral Cockburn was having a merry time of it. For some reason he insisted on riding through the streets on an unkempt white mare, followed by its little foal. When some of the women approached him and begged him not to burn their homes, he answered cheerfully, "Never fear, you shall be much safer under my administration than Madison's."

Having overseen the destruction of most of the public buildings, the admiral decided it was time for a little personal revenge. He had not forgotten the scathing articles printed about "the monster Cockburn" in the *National Intelligencer*. And he had not forgiven the newspaper's publisher, Joseph Gales. He would relish seeing that building burn to the ground. But he was stopped by some ladies in the crowd.

> When he went to burn Mr. Gale's office, whom he called his "dear Josey"; Mrs. Brush, Mrs. Stelle and a few citizens remonstrated with him, assuring him that it would occasion the loss of all the buildings in the row. "Well," said he, "good people I do not wish to injure you, but I am really afraid my friend Josey will be affronted with me, if after burning Jemmy's palace, I do not pay him the same compliment."

They reached a compromise. Instead of burning the building, Cockburn ordered it pulled down.

Heavy ropes were passed through the windows and tied around the walls. It took the men less than two hours of pulling to flatten the building to the ground. After that, they heaped paper, files, and printing presses in piles and burned them. Even the letters of type were thrown into the flames.

"I went to look at the ruins of the President's house. The rooms which you saw, so richly furnished, exhibited nothing but unroofed naked walls, cracked, defaced and blackened with fire. I cannot tell you what I felt as I walked amongst them."

—William Wirt, Washington resident, in a letter to his wife, October 14, 1814

Admiral Cockburn supervised the destruction. "Be sure that all the C's are destroyed," he joked, "so that the rascals can have no further means of abusing my name as they have done."

A crowd of ladies was standing nearby and came forward to meet the admiral, not realizing who he was. In conversation they found him charming. One stopped Lieutenant Scott and asked for the name of the "delightful officer." "Why, that is the vile monster, Cock-burn," he replied, pronouncing the name in the American way. "A half-uttered shriek of terror escaped from the lips of some of them, as the dreaded name tingled on their ears."

Admiral Cockburn himself seemed to enjoy teasing the ladies with his frightening reputation. "He stop'd at a door, at which a young lady was standing and enter'd into familiar conversation. 'Now did you expect to see me such a clever fellow,' said he, 'were you not prepared to see a savage, a ferocious creature, such as Josey represented me? But you see I am quite harmless, don't be afraid, I will take better care of you than Jemmy did!'"

"James Madison is a rascal, a coward and a fool."

—Graffiti scrawled on ruined walls of the Capitol

The "clever fellow" had every reason to be in a jaunty mood. The past twenty-four hours had been a splendid success. Nearly everything had gone exactly according to plan for the British invaders. It would be hard for the gleeful admiral to imagine what could go wrong now.

A New Tempest

The explosion shook the ground and stopped the residents of Washington in their tracks. Many took cover, believing that the two sides were firing cannons at each other again.

The blast—at Greenleaf's Point, about two miles from the Capitol—was deafening. It carved a crater twenty feet deep and twice as wide. The force flattened some nearby buildings and ripped the roofs clean off others.

And then there were the bodies. Thirty British soldiers were killed instantly, some blown to bits. Others were buried alive beneath the enormous wall of debris that had been thrown up. The wounded lay crushed and twisted. Severed limbs were everywhere. One shaken officer wrote home that the gruesome scene was "a thousand times more distressing than the loss we met with in the field [at Bladensburg] the day before."

That morning the troops had gone to the fort at Greenleaf's Point to destroy any ammunition there. Lieutenant Scott explained what happened:

A large quantity of [gun]powder was found, and, in order to effect its destruction with safety, it was thrown down a well of tolerable depth, though not full of water. . . . So many barrels of powder had been deposited in it, that the casks and loose powder soon rested above the water line; it was unfortunately not reported by the workmen to the officer superintending the duty, and they continued rolling cask after cask down the abyss. An awful explosion took place, caused, it is supposed, by the sparks of fire emitted by the striking of the barrels in their descent against the stony sides of the well.

Young Michael Shiner had a different explanation: "The British armmy wher taking ther last round in the city of Washington and puting on a great Many airs . . . smoking of others segars [cigars] and throing them about then threw some down a Well where there wher some powder throed down ther by the american people."

Whether the cause was sparks or "segars," Dr. Ewell spent the next few days tending to the horribly injured men.

As if one catastrophe were not enough for the day, a violent storm hit the still-reeling city around noon. It may have been a tornado or a hurricane, or a tornado spawned by a hurricane. Whatever it was, it was the worst storm even the oldest residents of Washington could remember.

The wind tore roofs off houses and lifted cannons off the ground. Soldiers who had been caught outside had to flatten themselves to the earth to keep from being blown away.

Lieutenant Gleig was on horseback when the storm struck. The wind picked him right out of the saddle and spooked his horse so badly he never saw it again.

I never listened to thunder more deafening, and its force was such as to throw down houses, tear up trees, and carry stones, beams of timber, and whole masses of brickwork, like feathers into the air. . . . The noise of the wind and the thunder, the crash of falling buildings, and the tearing of roofs as they were stript from the walls, produced the most appalling effect I ever have, and probably ever shall, witness.

The storm lasted nearly two hours. Thirty British soldiers who had survived the battle the day before—and the gunpowder explosion that morning—were buried under the rubble of buildings torn apart by wind.

Later that afternoon Admiral Cockburn came upon a woman in front of her house. He spluttered, "Great God, Madam! Is this the kind of storm to which you are accustomed in this infernal country?"

The woman answered back that, no, it was a special punishment from heaven "to drive our enemies from our city."

"Not so, Madam," he replied, "it is rather to aid your enemies in the destruction of your city."

And Then They Were Gone

Admiral Cockburn and General Ross sat out the storm in Dr. Ewell's home, which they had seized as their headquarters. They had already accomplished all they had set out to do, and more. Their men were exhausted and still jittery from the day's shocking losses. Besides, there were rumors that American troops were rallying in greater numbers. It was a good time to leave.

Secrecy was vital; they did not want to risk being followed. An eight o'clock curfew was declared for that evening. All residents of Washington were to stay indoors on pain of death. In the darkness

British troops silently prepared to withdraw from the capital they had fought so hard to invade.

Lieutenant Gleig described the preparations:

> All the horses belonging to different officers were removed . . . , no one being allowed to ride, lest a neigh, or even the trampling of hoofs, should excite suspicion. The [watch]fires were trimmed, and made to blaze brightly; fuel enough was left to keep them so for some hours; and finally, about half past nine o'clock the troops formed in marching order, and moved off in the most profound silence. Not a word was spoken, nor a single individual permitted to step one inch out of his place, by which means they passed along the streets perfectly unnoticed, and cleared the town without any alarm being given.

The ruse was a success. Even Michael Shiner, who didn't miss much, heard nothing. (He speculated that the British must have muffled the horses' hooves to keep them quiet.) When the residents of Washington awoke the next morning, they were astonished to find that the British had disappeared in the night. The entire occupation had lasted just over twenty-four hours. The young slave summed up the invasion in his usual colorful way: "The commander of the British squadron in 1814 that came up to the potomac river didnt act no Ways like a gentelman . . . for the Worst of hetheans wouldent of acted anny More heatheanly then he did."

"A veteran host by veterans led,
With Ross and Cockburn at
  their head,
They came—they saw—they
  burned—and fled!"
—Poet Philip Freneau

Francis Scott Key's poem "The Star-Spangled Banner," written on the back of a letter. The original manuscript is on display at the Maryland Historical Society.

Chapter Nine

And After

To Fight Another Day

Had it happened in modern times, Admiral Cockburn might have called a press conference aboard his flagship, the *Albion*. There might have been reporters and cameras and a banner proclaiming "Mission Accomplished." In view of the smoking piles of rubble left behind in Washington, any gloating would have been understandable. The burning of the capital, however, was not the end of the war—and it is not the end of this story.

After leaving Washington, British troops headed north to attack the busy port city of Baltimore. But Baltimore was no Bladensburg. This time thousands of American militiamen stood their ground. They blocked the path to the city, forcing the British to attempt an invasion by sea instead. And to do that they had to get past Fort McHenry. All through the day of September 13 and throughout that night, British bomb ships pounded the fort with shells and rockets. The next morning, when Francis Scott Key saw the American flag flying triumphantly over the fort "by dawn's early light," it marked more than the birth of the national anthem. It marked a turning point in the war. Forced back by both land and sea, the British had no choice but to retreat.

But that was not the end of the war, either.

On Christmas Eve 1814, four months to the day after the invasion of Washington, British and American representatives signed a peace treaty in Ghent, Belgium. Neither side gained or lost much in the agreement. Any land seized had to be returned. None of the issues that had so infuriated war hawks, including the impressment of American sailors, were addressed. It was simply agreed that all fighting would stop and everything would go back to the way it had been.

But even that was not the end of the war.

It took weeks for news of the treaty to make its way across the Atlantic. By the time the first rumors of peace reached the United States, British and American troops had already squared off in battle at New Orleans. The outcome was almost unbelievably lopsided. On January 8, 1815, more than two thousand British soldiers were killed, wounded, or went missing in the battle. Only thirteen Americans lost their lives, and another fifty-eight were wounded or missing. The victory stunned even the victors.

The Battle of New Orleans was the last major battle of the war. On February 16, 1815, the US Senate approved the treaty with Britain. The next day, President Madison signed it. The war was at last over.

A celebration of the Treaty of Ghent. The figures at bottom represent the United States and Great Britain, holding hands in friendship. The dove at top is a symbol of peace.

Curtain Calls

After the burning of Washington, Admiral George Cockburn boasted, "I do not believe a Vestage of Public Property, or a Store of any kind which could be converted to the use of the Government, escaped Destruction." His success in torching the capital of the United States added luster to an already illustrious career. He eventually rose to become a member of Parliament as well as the head of the Royal Navy. In the eyes of the British, he was nothing less than a national hero.

At home James Madison was blamed for the invasion of the capital and the burning of Washington. Political cartoons depicted him as a coward scurrying away from the capital, buildings ablaze behind him. But just six months later, he was hailed as a hero for bringing the war to a close. James ended his term more popular than when he had started, and retired to his lifelong home in Virginia in 1817.

After the events of August 24, Dolley Madison was more beloved than ever. The story of how she saved the painting of George Washington became part of her legend. Unfortunately, shortly after James's death in 1836, money troubles forced her into near poverty. She was compelled to sell Montpelier, all its furniture, and most of its slaves. She returned to Washington, where she found she had lost none of her popularity. When she died in 1849, her funeral procession was one of the largest in Washington history.

Just days after "the Bladensburg Races" and the invasion of Washington, Secretary of War John Armstrong was forced by the president to resign. He left Washington in disgrace. To his dying day he refused to accept any responsibility for the invasion and the destruction of the nation's capital.

General Robert Ross did not live to see the peace. Less than three weeks after the burning of Washington, he was killed at the Battle of Baltimore. His body was sealed in a keg of rum to preserve it and shipped to Nova Scotia for burial.

Lieutenant George Gleig had interrupted his college studies to become a soldier. After the war he went back to school and eventually became an Anglican minister, though he never stopped writing about life in the military.

After his adventures in the war, Private John Pendleton Kennedy became a writer and published several successful novels. He also took up a career as a politician. He was elected to Congress and even served as secretary of the navy for a short time.

Paul Jennings remained a slave in the Madison household and was with James when he died. Afterward he might have expected Dolley to free him. Instead, he was sold for two hundred dollars. A short time later he was bought by Senator Daniel Webster, from whom he purchased his freedom at age forty-eight. He later wrote down his recollections of life as a slave in the President's House. His book, published in 1865 as *A Colored Man's Reminiscences of James Madison*, is the first known White House memoir.

Michael Shiner spent his early adult years as a slave working in the paint shop at the rebuilt Washington Navy Yard. Eight years after his master's death in 1832, Shiner became a free man. Speaking of his freedom, he said proudly, "The only master I have now is the Constitution."

Mordecai Booth kept his position as clerk at the Washington Navy Yard for many years. Commodore Thomas Tingey served as commandant of the yard until his death in 1829. To this day his ghost is said to haunt the Commandant's Quarters, one of the few buildings not burned in 1814.

Political cartoons poked fun at the president after the burning of Washington. This British one shows James Madison and Secretary of War John Armstrong fleeing the burning city, clutching papers as they run.

And the White House? Talk of rebuilding began almost immediately. While some people thought the fires were an opportunity to move the capital to a grander city, most felt that doing so would be another victory for the British. The capital—and the President's House—would stay put. James Madison insisted that the White House be rebuilt exactly as it had stood, and the original designer

The White House restored. The South Portico, or columned porch, was added in 1824.

was hired to see that this was done. James and Dolley found other accommodations while the rebuilding took place.

The project took three years. In October 1817 a new president, James Monroe, moved in, though the plaster walls were still wet and the woodwork unpainted. On New Year's Day 1818, the refurbished White House had its public debut. Three thousand people crowded

in to see the restored house with its grand French furnishings, silver, porcelain, and other splendors. The portrait of George Washington was returned to its place on the wall. The *National Intelligencer* cheered, "It was gratifying to be able once more to salute the President of the United States with the compliments of the season in his appropriate residence."

The White House was back.

A Mouse No Longer

Admiral Cockburn had indeed avenged the destruction of York in Canada, as he had set out to do. But if his mission was to restore the former colony to the Crown and see the United States as a brief hiccup in the history of Great Britain, he failed.

Something happened to the American people after "the second war of independence." Somehow they saw themselves differently. They saw that they had gone toe to toe with the greatest naval power in the world and had held their own. Some, hearing the news of the Battle of New Orleans at the same time as news of the peace treaty, believed that the United States had trounced the British. It had not, of course.

But it hadn't lost, either. From now on, the American flag would be honored and respected around the world. The American people saw that the United States was no longer an infant nation. It was growing up.

As he had gazed at the ruins of the Capitol on the night of August 24, 1814, eighteen-year-old Lieutenant Gleig had laughed at the impudence of these Americans. The Capitol stood on a hill near a little stream that they had named the Tiber—after the great river that flowed through ancient Rome. He scoffed, "These modern republicans are led to flatter themselves that the days are coming when [their Capitol] will rival in power and grandeur the Senate-house of ancient Rome herself."

Gleig could not have known how true his words would prove to be. The day was coming when the United States would eclipse even the mighty Great Britain in power. In time, the nation's reach and influence would indeed be as great as that of ancient Rome—or greater. In modern times, it would be called a superpower.

One of the most important signs of its power is the White House. More than just the president's home, the White House is an enduring symbol of the presidency, the government, and the nation itself. Its familiar exterior is recognized throughout the world.

Looking at that proud exterior, few would guess that the events of August 24, 1814, had ever happened. But below the now-familiar columned entrance, on an archway leading into an old kitchen, on blocks of stone that were once part of the original walls, the black scars of scorch marks still remain today.

They tell their own tale of what happened that night.

Acknowledgments

This book began as a tiny seed of an idea. I owe a great deal to all those who nurtured it to full maturity.

Thanks first to my editor at Charlesbridge, Alyssa Mito Pusey, for her enthusiastic support of the project in its early stages and for her expert skill in shaping and tightening the finished text. She has the gift of knowing how to deal not just with the printed word but with the author whose baby it is.

Many thanks to Diane Earley, associate art director at Charlesbridge, who threw herself heart and soul into this project. This book owes much to her vision.

I was honored to be given a tour of areas of the White House normally off-limits to the public, and especially to be allowed to see the 1814 burn marks for myself. Thanks to Monica McKiernan, White House curatorial assistant, who arranged the tour, and to Lydia Tederick, White House assistant curator, who conducted it and patiently answered my questions.

I am especially indebted to William Seale, historian and author of *The President's House: A History,* who read the text and gave his expert opinion.

As always, thanks to my critique group partners, Pat Aust, Joan Horton, and Joyce Stengel. They always knew just what needed tweaking.

Most of all, thanks to my husband, Skip. Who else would have endured being dragged around Washington's Congressional Cemetery on a hunt for gravestones in one-hundred-degree heat without complaint?

Sources of Quotations

Please see the bibliography on pages 114–116 for more information about the cited works.

Chapter One

p. 1: "On the opening . . . servants." Margaret Bayard Smith, *The First Forty Years of Washington Society*, p. 99.

p. 4: "The enemy . . . the men." *National Intelligencer*, June 17, 1813.

p. 4: "monster" and "disgrace . . . human race." *National Intelligencer*, June 25, 1813.

p. 4: "Houseburn." *National Intelligencer*, June 30, 1813.

p. 4: "Admiral Cockburn . . . benefit from it." *National Intelligencer*, June 17, 1813.

p. 7: "A certain . . . delivery." *Niles' Register*, August 21, 1813, quoted in James Pack, *The Man Who Burned the White House*, p. 155.

p. 7: "We had . . . cruelty." Christian Hines, *Early Recollections of Washington City*, p. 57.

pp. 7–8: "Now all . . . country." Miss Brown quoted in Anne Hollingsworth Wharton, *Social Life in the Early Republic*, p. 163.

p. 8: "busy packing." Eleanor Jones quoted in Catherine Allgor, *A Perfect Union*, p. 311.

p. 8: "Oh yes! . . . consequence." John Armstrong quoted by John van Ness to Richard M. Johnson, *American State Papers*, p. 581.

p. 9: "Genl. Armstrong . . . Government." Stephen Pleasonton in a letter to William Winder, August 7, 1848, quoted in John C. Hildt, "Letters Relating to the Capture of Washington," *South Atlantic Quarterly*, p. 65.

p. 10: "As we . . . real war." John Pendleton Kennedy quoted in Henry T. Tuckerman, *The Life of John Pendleton Kennedy*, pp. 71–72.

p. 10: "very dashy uniform." Ibid., p. 65.

p. 10: "after we . . . ready for it." Ibid., pp. 74–75.

pp. 10–11: "Every one . . . cross-belts." Ibid., p. 78.

p. 11: "We had . . . move on." Ibid., p. 79.

p. 13: "The orders . . . immediately." James Scott, *Recollections of a Naval Life*, pp. 281–282.

p. 14: "No . . . retreat" and "I'll . . . go on." George Cockburn quoted in Scott, p. 283.

Chapter Two

pp. 17–18: "Dear Sister…private." Dolley Madison in a letter to Lucy Payne Washington Todd, August 23, 1814, in Dolley Madison, *Memoirs and Letters of Dolley Madison, Wife of James Madison, President of the United States*, p. 33. Dolley's original letter was most likely lost or destroyed. She recreated it many years later.

p. 18: "Presidentess." *National Intelligencer*, March 4, 1809, found in Allgor, p. 144.

p. 19: "Our hearts . . . other." Dolley Madison in a letter to James Madison, October 23, 1815, in D. Madison, p. 18.

p. 19: "She really . . . royalty." M. B. Smith, p. 62.

p. 19: "I never . . . appears to be." Catharine Akerly Mitchill quoted in Allgor, p. 174.

p. 21: "It was scarcely . . . indeed." M. B. Smith, p. 61.

p. 21: "As we entered . . . unnoticed." Miss Brown quoted in Wharton, p. 163.

p. 21: "Everybody loves . . . everybody." Conversation between Henry Clay and Dolley Madison quoted in Cokie Roberts, *Ladies of Liberty*, p. 189.

p. 23: "a smile . . . everybody." Washington Irving quoted in Allgor, p. 250.

p. 23: "The windows . . . $4.00 a yard." Elbridge Gerry Jr. quoted in Roberts, p. 261.

p. 23: "I was . . . Mr. Madison alone." Charles Cotesworth Pinckney quoted in Richard N. Cote, *Strength and Honor*, p. 251.

p. 24: "The reports . . . represented." James Madison in a letter to Dolley Madison, August 13, 1814 in James Madison, *The Writings of James Madison*, pp. 293–294.

p. 24: "The last . . . destroying it." Dolley Madison in a letter to Lucy Payne Washington Todd, August 23, 1814, in D. Madison, p. 33.

p. 24: "make his bow." Dolley Madison in a letter to Edward Coles, May 12, 1813, in D. Madison, p. 28.

p. 24: "unless she . . . her head." George Cockburn quoted in D. Madison, p. 31.

p. 25: "I . . . within reach." Dolley Madison in a letter to Edward Coles, May 12, 1813, in D. Madison, p. 28.

p. 25: "I am . . . safe." Dolley Madison in a letter to Lucy Payne Washington Todd, August 23, 1814, in D. Madison, p. 33.

p. 25: "a complete drubbing." Alexander Cochrane quoted in Anthony S. Pitch, *The Burning of Washington*, p. 147.

Chapter Three

p. 27: "cool and agreeable." George Robert Gleig, *The Campaigns of the British Army at Washington and New Orleans, in the Years 1814–1815,* p. 61.

p. 27: "enthusiastically attached." Ibid., p. 2.

p. 28: "One wish . . . their [ambushes]." George Robert Gleig, *A Subaltern in America*, p. 34.

p. 28: "The Americans . . . ten minutes." Ibid., p. 33.

p. 28: "whether they . . . reply." Gleig, *Campaigns*, p. 56.

p. 28: "In these . . . British." Allen McClane, "Journal of the Campaign," in *Notices of the War of 1812* by John Armstrong, p. 236.

p. 29: "Slung over . . . my back." Gleig, *Subaltern*, p. 10.

p. 29: "I do not . . . keep up." Gleig, *Campaigns*, p. 61.

pp. 29–30: "The ashes . . . night here." Gleig, *Subaltern*, p. 64.

p. 32: "He said . . . beaten." James Madison in a memorandum written August 24, 1814, in J. Madison, p. 295.

pp. 32–33: "We had . . . left behind." Gleig, *Campaigns*, p. 63.

p. 33: "My eyes . . . the ground." Gleig, *Subaltern*, p. 65.

p. 33: "some of . . . go on." Gleig, *Campaigns*, p. 63.

p. 33: "[The British] were . . . swords." *National Intelligencer*, August 31, 1814.

Chapter Four

p. 35: "Wednesday Morning . . . fireside." Dolley Madison in a letter to Lucy Payne Washington Todd, August 23, 1814, in D. Madison, pp. 33–34.

p. 36: "nine thousand . . . attack them." Gleig, *Campaigns*, p. 64.

p. 36: "We feel . . . the city." *National Intelligencer*, August 24, 1814.

p. 37: "A few . . . green hill." Gleig, *Subaltern*, p. 67.

p. 37: "I have . . . no words." Ibid., pp. 67–68.

p. 39: "The word . . . bridge." Gleig, *Campaigns*, p. 65.

Chapter Five

p. 42: "They look . . . artillery." General Wittgenstein, probably General Peter Ludwig Wittgenstein, quoted in Gareth Glover, "History of the Rocket—1804 to 1815," *Napoleonic Literature*, p. 6. (Glover gives his source for the quote as *Edinburgh Evening Courant*, January 20, 1814.)

p. 44: "A gallant soldier . . . wee bit.'" Scott, p. 286.

p. 44: "'Forward . . . word heard." Gleig, *Subaltern*, p. 71.

p. 44: "The fire . . . cannon." Henry Fulford quoted in William M. Marine, *The British Invasion of Maryland, 1812–1815*, p. 114.

p. 45: "Our troops . . . victors." Gleig, *Campaigns*, pp. 65–66.

p. 45: "They were . . . whole of us." Henry Fulford quoted in Marine, p. 114.

p. 45: "Never did . . . their legs." Gleig, *Subaltern*, p. 71.

p. 46: "The rout . . . galloped off." Gleig, *Campaigns*, pp. 66–67.

p. 46: "We made . . . it." John Pendleton Kennedy quoted in Tuckerman, p. 79.

p. 46: "one of . . . do it." Paul Jennings, *A Colored Man's Reminiscences of James Madison*, p. 15.

pp. 46–48: "was beloved . . . the house." Ibid., p. 14.

p. 48: "Every thing . . . intentions." Ibid., p. 7.

p. 48: "Three o'clock . . . protect us!" Dolley Madison in a letter to Lucy Payne Washington Todd, August 23, 1814, in D. Madison, p. 34.

pp. 48–49: "James Smith . . . confusion." Jennings, pp. 8–9.

p. 49: "Here . . . wait for him." Dolley Madison in a letter to Lucy Payne Washington Todd, August 23, 1814, in D. Madison, p. 34.

p. 49: "I lost . . . mine." John Pendleton Kennedy quoted in Tuckerman, pp. 79–80.

p. 49: "Oh how . . . gone." M. B. Smith, p. 101.

p. 50: "'Poh! poh! . . . excellent!'" Scott, pp. 288–289.

p. 53: "Of the sailors . . . the field." Gleig, *Campaigns*, p. 67.

p. 53: "They have . . . had." George Cockburn quoted in Louis Arthur Norton, *Joshua Barney*, p. 183.

pp. 53–54: "I soon . . . at hand!'" James Ewell quoted in M. I. Weller, "Unwelcome Visitors to Washington, August 24, 1814," in *Records of the Columbia Historical Society, Washington, DC*, p. 7.

p. 54: "The raw militiamen . . . enemy." Ibid., p. 10.

pp. 54–55: "Our kind friend . . . wall" and "I have . . . safe keeping." Dolley Madison in a letter to Lucy Payne Washington Todd, August 23, 1814, in D. Madison, p. 34.

p. 55: "I confess . . . window . . ." Dolley Madison in a letter to Mary Latrobe, December 3, 1814, in Allen C. Clark, *Life and Letters of Dolly* [sic] *Madison*, p. 166.

p. 55: "And now . . . cannot tell!" Dolley Madison in a letter to Lucy Payne Washington Todd, August 23, 1814, in D. Madison, p. 34.

p. 57: "A rabble . . . hands on." Jennings, pp. 9–10.

p. 57: "crowned . . . went off." George Cockburn in a report to Alexander Cochrane, August 27, 1814, in "The Defense and Burning of Washington in 1814: Naval Documents of the War of 1812," *The Navy Department Library.*

p. 57: "The red coats . . . *long run.*" Assistant Postmaster General William H. Dundas to clerk (and militiaman) John Smith, quoted in Horatio King, "The Battle of Bladensburg: Burning of Washington in 1814," *Magazine of American History with Notes and Queries*, p. 438. Italics in original.

Chapter Six

p. 60: "for ages to come." William Seale, *The President's House: A History*, p. 21.

p. 60: "Passing over . . . unornamented grounds." Miss Brown quoted in Wharton, p. 161.

p. 60: "We frequented . . . path." Louisa Adams quoted in Roberts, p. 110.

p. 60: "[Washington was] a meagre . . . swamps." Richard Rush quoted in Pitch, p. 29.

p. 62: "Waggons and Men . . . confusion." Mordecai Booth to Thomas Tingey, August 24, 1814, in "The Defense and Burning of Washington."

pp. 62–63: "I saw not . . . pannick struck." Ibid.

p. 63: "No time . . . the yard." Thomas Tingey to William Jones, August 27, 1814, in "The Defense and Burning of Washington."

pp. 63–64: "I saw . . . their doors," "by which . . . done," "He Seem'd . . . Pistol," "[He] Dismounted . . . Church," and "Then . . . fate." Mordecai Booth to Thomas Tingey, August 24, 1814, in "The Defense and Burning of Washington."

p. 65: "As son [soon] . . . spanish dollar." Michael Shiner, "The Diary of Michael Shiner Relating to the History of the Washington Navy Yard, 1813–1869," *The Navy Department Library*, p. 6. "[Vermillion]" in the original transcription.

Chapter Seven

p. 69: "I passed . . . the Yard." Mordecai Booth to Thomas Tingey, August 24, 1814, in "The Defense and Burning of Washington."

p. 69: "Admiral Cockburn . . . public buildings." Harry George Wakelyn Smith, *The Autobiography of Lieutenant-General Sir Harry Smith, Baronet of Aliwal on the Sutlej, G.C.B.*, p. 200.

p. 70: "In a twinkale . . . east and West." Shiner, p. 7. "[Firing?]" in the original transcription.

pp. 70–71: "an edifice . . . elegant." Gleig, *Campaigns*, p. 74.

p. 71: "Each of . . . young nation." Scott, pp. 300–301.

p. 72: "Shall this . . . aye." George Cockburn quoted in Charles J. Ingersoll, *Historical Sketch of the Second War Between the United States of America and Great Britain*, p. 185.

p. 72: "Its funereal . . . hour of ten." Scott, p. 301.

pp. 72–73: "Taken . . . Governor of Bermuda." George Cockburn quoted in Pitch, p. 108.

p. 73: "I had . . . President's house." H. G. W. Smith, p. 200.

p. 73: "Never shall . . . gloom." James Ewell quoted in Weller, p. 11.

p. 73: "A noble library . . . spared." Gleig, *Campaigns*, p. 70.

p. 74: "a whole week . . . fright." Barbara Suter quoted in Ingersoll, p. 186.

p. 77: "Instead of . . . the grate." Gleig, *Campaigns*, pp. 71–72.

p. 77: "the little president" and "keep Dolley . . . London." British soldier quoted in Pitch, page 118.

p. 78: "[Cockburn] insisted . . . something too." M. B. Smith, pp. 111–112.

p. 78: "Jemmy's." Ibid., p. 111.

p. 78: "seat." George Cockburn quoted in Allgor, p. 316.

p. 78: "Passing through . . . United States." Scott, p. 304.

pp. 78–79: "Each [carried] . . . the blaze!" M. B. Smith, p. 111.

p. 79: "Our sailors . . . work." H. G. W. Smith, p. 200.

p. 81: "It will . . . require rest." Robert Ross quoted in Ingersoll, p. 186.

p. 82: "You never . . . the city." Washington resident Mary Hunter quoted in Pitch, p. 124.

pp. 82–83: "I have . . . dark horizon." Richard Rush quoted in John S. Williams, *History of the Invasion and Capture of Washington, and the Events Which Preceded and Followed*, p. 274.

p. 83: "In the evening . . . fire." Jennings, pp. 10–11.

p. 83: "The conflagration . . . awful." James Ewell quoted in Weller, p. 8.

p. 83: "large portion . . . public buildings." Miss Brown quoted in Wharton, p. 173.

p. 83: "A sight . . . so Awful." Mordecai Booth to Thomas Tingey, August 24, 1814, in "The Defense and Burning of Washington."

p. 83: "At first . . . not to cry." Matilda Roberts quoted in Roberts, p. 273.

Chapter Eight

p. 87: "Thursday morning . . . event!" M. B. Smith, p. 100.

p. 87: "The state . . . from me." M. B. Smith, p. 103.

p. 88: "Never fear . . . Madison's." George Cockburn quoted in Ingersoll, p. 189.

p. 88: "When he . . . compliment.'" M. B. Smith, p. 112.

p. 89: "Be sure . . . have done." George Cockburn quoted in King, p. 453.

p. 89: "delightful officer . . . their ears." Scott, p. 308.

p. 89: "He stop'd . . . Jemmy did!'" M. B. Smith, p. 112.

p. 89: "I went . . . amongst them." William Wirt in a letter to his wife, Elizabeth Washington, presumably Elizabeth Washington Wirt once married, quoted in King, p. 451.

p. 90: "James Madison . . . fool." Graffiti quoted in Pitch, p. 163.

p. 90: "a thousand . . . day before." British officer quoted in Pitch, p. 138. Brackets in the original.

pp. 90–91: "A large quantity . . . well." Scott, pp. 312–313.

p. 91: "The British . . . american people." Shiner, p. 8.

pp. 91–92: "I never . . . witness." Gleig, *Subaltern*, p. 85; *Campaigns*, p. 76.

p. 92: "Great God . . . your city." Conversation between George Cockburn and Washington resident quoted in Pitch, p. 142.

p. 93: "All the horses . . . being given." Gleig, *Campaigns*, p. 78.

p. 93: "The commander . . . he did." Shiner, p. 9.

p. 93: "A veteran host . . . fled!" Philip Freneau quoted in King, p. 455.

Chapter Nine

p. 98: "I do not . . . Destruction." George Cockburn in a report to Alexander Cochrane, August 27, 1814, in "The Defense and Burning of Washington."

p. 99: "The only master . . . Constitution." Shiner, preface.

p. 104: "It was gratifying . . . appropriate residence." *National Intelligencer*, January 3, 1818, found in Seale, p. 149.

p. 105: "These modern . . . Rome herself." Gleig, *Campaigns*, p. 74.

Bibliography

Allgor, Catherine. *A Perfect Union: Dolley Madison and the Creation of the American Nation.* New York: Henry Holt, 2010.

American State Papers: Documents, Legislative and Executive, of the Congress of the United States. Class V: Military Affairs. Vol. 1. http://memory.loc.gov/ammem /amlaw/lwsplink.html.

"The Burning of the White House in 1814." *White House History* 4 (fall 1998). Reprinted in *White House History: Collection 1, Numbers 1 Through 6.* Washington, DC: White House Historical Association, 2004.

Clark, Allen C. *Life and Letters of Dolly* [sic] *Madison.* Washington, DC: Press of W. F. Roberts Company, 1914.

Cote, Richard N. *Strength and Honor: The Life of Dolley Madison.* Mt. Pleasant, SC: Corinthian Books, 2005.

"The Defense and Burning of Washington in 1814: Naval Documents of the War of 1812." *The Navy Department Library.* http://www.history.navy.mil/library/online /burning_washington.htm.

Gleig, George Robert. *The Campaigns of the British Army at Washington and New Orleans, in the Years 1814–1815.* London: John Murray, 1827.

———. *A Subaltern in America: Comprising His Narrative of the Campaign of the British Army at Baltimore, Washington, &c, &c During the Late War.* Philadelphia: E. L. Carey and A. Hart, 1833.

Glover, Gareth. "History of the Rocket—1804 to 1815." *Napoleonic Literature.* http://web.archive.org/web/20081223042129/http://www.napoleonic-literature.com /Articles/Rockets/History_of_Rockets.htm.

Haythornthwaite, Philip J. *Wellington's Army: The Uniforms of the British Soldier, 1812–1815.* Mechanicsburg, PA: Stackpole Books, 2002.

Hibben, Henry B. *Navy Yard, Washington: History from Organization, 1799, to Present Date.* Washington, DC: Government Printing Office, 1890. This was the source of the eventual whereabouts of Mordecai Booth.

Hildt, John C. "Letters Relating to the Capture of Washington." *South Atlantic Quarterly* 6 (1907): 58–66.

Hines, Christian. *Early Recollections of Washington City.* Washington, DC: Junior League of Washington, 1981. First published 1866 by the Columbia Historical Society.

Ingersoll, Charles J. *Historical Sketch of the Second War Between the United States of America and Great Britain.* Vol. 2. Philadelphia: Lea and Blanchard, 1849.

James, William. *A Full and Correct Account of the Military Occurrences of the Late War Between Great Britain and the United States of America.* Vol. 2. London: Black, Kingsbury, Parbury & Allen, 1818.

Jennings, Paul. *A Colored Man's Reminiscences of James Madison.* Brooklyn, NY: George C. Beadle, 1865.

"Joshua Barney and the Battle of Bladensburg, War of 1812." *Barney Family Historical Association.* http://www.barneyfamily.org/docs/article_03.php.

King, Horatio. "The Battle of Bladensburg: Burning of Washington in 1814." *Magazine of American History with Notes and Queries* 14 (July–December 1885): 438–457.

Langguth, A. J. *Union 1812: The Americans Who Fought the Second War of Independence.* New York: Simon & Schuster, 2006.

Madison, Dolley. *Memoirs and Letters of Dolley Madison, Wife of James Madison, President of the United States.* Memphis, TN: General Books, 2010.

Madison, James. *The Writings of James Madison.* Vol. 8. Edited by Gaillard Hunt. New York: G. P. Putnam's Sons, 1908.

Marine, William M. *The British Invasion of Maryland, 1812–1815.* Baltimore, MD: John H. Saumenig, 1913.

McClane, Allen. "Journal of the Campaign." In *Notices of the War of 1812,* vol. 2, by John Armstrong, 232–236. New York: Wiley & Putnam, 1840.

Norton, Louis Arthur. *Joshua Barney: Hero of the Revolution and 1812.* Annapolis, MD: Naval Institute Press, 2000.

Pack, James. *The Man Who Burned the White House: Admiral Sir George Cockburn, 1772–1853.* Emsworth, Hampshire: Kenneth Mason, 1987.

Peck, Taylor. *Round-Shot to Rockets: A History of the Washington Navy Yard and U.S. Naval Gun Factory.* Annapolis, MD: United States Naval Institute, 1949.

Pitch, Anthony S. *The Burning of Washington: The British Invasion of 1814.* Annapolis, MD: Naval Institute Press, 2000.

Richardson, James D. "James Madison." Vol, 1, part 4, of *A Compilation of the Messages and Papers of the Presidents.* Public Domain Books, 2004.

Roberts, Cokie. *Ladies of Liberty: The Women Who Shaped Our Nation.* New York: HarperCollins e-books, 2008.

Scott, James. *Recollections of a Naval Life.* Vol. 3. London: Richard Bentley, 1834.

Seale, William. *The President's House: A History.* Vol. 1. Washington, DC: White House Historical Association with the cooperation of The National Geographic Society, 1986.

Shiner, Michael. "The Diary of Michael Shiner Relating to the History of the Washington Navy Yard, 1813–1869." Transcribed with introduction and notes by John G. Sharp. *The Navy Department Library*. October 12, 2007. http://www.history. navy .mil/library/online/shinerdiary.html#page3.

Shulman, Holly C., ed. *The Dolley Madison Digital Edition*. Charlottesville, VA: University of Virginia Press, Rotunda, version 2009.06. http://rotunda.upress .virginia.edu/dmde.

Smith, Harry George Wakelyn. *The Autobiography of Lieutenant-General Sir Harry Smith, Baronet of Aliwal on the Sutlej, G.C.B.* London: J. Murray, 1902.

Smith, Margaret Bayard. *The First Forty Years of Washington Society*. Edited by Gaillard Hunt. New York: Charles Scribner's Sons, 1906.

Taylor, Elizabeth Dowling. *A Slave in the White House: Paul Jennings and the Madisons*. New York: Palgrave Macmillan, 2012.

Tuckerman, Henry T. *The Life of John Pendleton Kennedy*. New York: G. P. Putnam & Sons, 1871.

Vineyard, Ron. "Stage Waggons and Coaches." *Colonial Williamsburg Digital Library*. August 2000. http://research.history.org/DigitalLibrary/View/index. cfm?doc= ResearchReports%5CRR0380.xml.

Warden, D. B. *A Chorographical and Statistical Description of the District of Columbia*. Paris: Smith, 1816.

Weller, M. I. "Unwelcome Visitors to Washington, August 24, 1814." In *Records of the Columbia Historical Society, Washington, DC,* vol. 1. Washington, DC: Columbia Historical Society, 1897.

Wharton, Anne Hollingsworth. *Social Life in the Early Republic*. Philadelphia and London: J. B. Lippincott Company, 1903.

Williams, John S. *History of the Invasion and Capture of Washington, and the Events Which Preceded and Followed*. New York: Harper & Brothers Publishers, 1857.

Winter, Frank H. *The First Golden Age of Rocketry*. Washington, DC: Smithsonian Institution Press, 1990.

Image Credits

Endsheets: Plans for the city of Washington, DC, by Andrew Ellicott (1792), courtesy of the Library of Congress.

Half title: View of the South Portico of the President's House as proposed by Benjamin Latrobe (1817), courtesy of the Library of Congress.

Title page: *The Taking of the City of Washington in America*, published by G. Thompson (London, 1814), courtesy of the Library of Congress.

p. vi: *Capture and Burning of Washington by the British, in 1814,* published in *Our First Century* by Richard Miller Devens (Springfield, MA: C. A. Nichols & Co., 1876), courtesy of the Library of Congress.

p. viii: *George Town and Federal City, or City of Washington*, print by T. Cartwright after a painting by George Beck (London and Philadelphia: Atkins & Nightingale, 1801), courtesy of the Library of Congress.

p. 3: *Impressment of American Seamen*, wood engraving after a painting by Howard Pyle, published in *Harper's Monthly* (April 1884), courtesy of the Library of Congress.

p. 6: *Rear-Admiral Sir George Cockburn, 1772–1853*, by John James Halls (ca. 1817) copyright © National Maritime Museum, Greenwich, London.

p. 12: Portrait of John Pendleton Kennedy published in *Cyclopaedia of American Literature* by Evert A. Duyckinck and George L. Duyckinck (New York: C. Scribner, 1855). HCL Widener, AL 1.71: Vol. 2: Image: J. P. Kennedy on pg. 220.

p. 16: Portrait of Dolley Payne Madison by Gilbert Stuart (1804), courtesy of the White House Historical Association (White House Collection).

p. 20: Portrait of James Madison by John Vanderlyn (1816), courtesy of the White House Historical Association (White House Collection).

p. 26: Portrait of George Gleig copyright © Shropshire Regimental Museum, Shrewsbury Castle.

p. 31: Portrait of William Winder by Charles Balthazar Julien Fevret de Saint-Mémin (1804), courtesy of the Library of Congress.

p. 34: *March of the British Army from Benedict to Bladensburg*, published in *The Pictorial Field-Book of the War of 1812* by Benson J. Lossing (New York: Harper & Brothers, 1869). Color added.

p. 38: Engraving of the bridge at Bladensburg published in *The Pictorial Field-Book of the War of 1812* by Benson J. Lossing (New York: Harper & Brothers, 1869).

p. 40: Plate 6 from *A Treatise on the General Principles, Powers and Facility of Application of the Congreve Rocket System as Compared with Artillery* by William Congreve (London: Longman, Rees, Orme, Brown, and Green, 1827), EC8.C7606.827t, Houghton Library, Harvard University.

p. 42: Plate 10 from *A Treatise on the General Principles, Powers and Facility of Application of the Congreve Rocket System as Compared with Artillery* by William Congreve (London: Longman, Rees, Orme, Brown, and Green, 1827), EC8.C7606.827t, Houghton Library, Harvard University.

p. 47: Daguerreotype of Paul Jennings courtesy of the Sylvia Jennings Alexander Estate and the Montpelier Foundation.

p. 51: Portrait of Joshua Barney published in *The Pictorial Field-Book of the War of 1812* by Benson J. Lossing (New York: Harper & Brothers, 1869).

p. 56: Portrait of George Washington by Gilbert Stuart (1797), courtesy of the White House Historical Association (White House Collection).

p. 58: *Washington in 1800* (1834), courtesy of the Library of Congress.

p. 66: *City of Washington from Beyond the Navy Yard*, engraving by W. J. Bennett after a painting by G. Cooke (New York: Lewis P. Clover, ca. 1834), courtesy of the Library of Congress.

p. 68: Painting of waterfront fire (probably the burning of the Washington Navy Yard) by William Thornton (1815), courtesy of the Library of Congress.

p. 71: *A View of the Capitol of Washington Before It Was Burnt Down by the British* by William Russell Birch (1800), courtesy of the Library of Congress.

pp. 74–75: Painting of the US Capitol by George Munger (1814), courtesy of the Library of Congress.

pp. 80–81: *A View of the Presidents House in the City of Washington After the Conflagration of the 24th August 1814*, hand-colored engraving by William Strickland after a painting by George Munger (1814), courtesy of the Library of Congress.

pp. 84–85: *Washington. [A] Representation of the Capture of the City of Washington, by the British Forces Under the Command of Major Genl. Ross and Rear Adml. Sir I. Cockburn, August 24th 1814, Wherein Are Shown, the Fort and the Flotilla*, published by I. Ryland (England, 1815), courtesy of the Library of Congress.

p. 86: *Cockburn in the Chair* by Alfred Fredericks (1814), courtesy of the Picture Collection, the New York Public Library, Astor, Lenox and Tilden Foundations.

p. 94: Original manuscript of "The Star-Spangled Banner" by Sir Francis Scott Key, courtesy of the Library of Congress.

p. 97: *Peace* by John Rubens Smith (ca. 1814), courtesy of the Library of Congress.

pp. 100–101: *The Fall of Washington—or Maddy in Full Flight* published by S. W. Fores (London, 1814), courtesy of the Library of Congress.

pp. 102–103: *Presidents House* by George Lehman (Washington, DC: Thompson & Homans, ca. 1830), courtesy of the Library of Congress.

Index